COLUMBIA UNIVERSITY PRESS

Publishers Since 1893

New York   Chichester, West Sussex

Copyright © 2002 Columbia University Press

All rights reserved

Library of Congress Cataloging-in-Publication Data

Scalia, Joseph.

Intimate violence : attacks upon psychic interiority / Joseph Scalia.

p.   cm.

Includes bibliographical references and index.

ISBN 0-231-11984-4 (cloth ; alk. paper)

1. Family violence—Prevention. 2. Abusive men—Psychology.

3. Wife abuse—Psychological aspects. 4. Family violence—Psychological aspects. I. Title.

RC569.5.F3 S27 2002

616.85'822—dc21

2001047365

Casebound editions of Columbia University Press books are printed

on permanent and durable acid-free paper.

Printed in the United States of America

Designed by Lisa Hamm

c 10 9 8 7 6 5 4 3 2 1

INTIMATE VIOLENCE

ATTACKS UPON PSYCHIC INTERIORITY

JOSEPH SCALIA

COLUMBIA UNIVERSITY PRESS   NEW YORK

INTIMATE VIOLENCE

CONTENTS

*I dedicate this book to my wife, Lynne
and my son, Joe
who never cease to move me*

ACKNOWLEDGMENTS

I t is rather eye-opening to contemplate those who have been instrumental in one way or another in the development of this book, from its conception all the way through to its final form.

I wish to thank, first of all, Ric Kumm, founder and therapist of M.A.N. (Men Advocating Nonviolence), who had the idea and gave me the chance to work with batterers in the first place. We had no idea how much we would be affected by our patients, how much they would spark us to think things we never would have guessed.

Victor Stampley was a depth-thinking psychotherapist who helped me see my way clear to trusting myself in the thick of things early on. A little later, William Ryan, a psychologist, helped me further to dare to think. These are the Montanans. And there have been many very conscientious and serious psychotherapists here who have provided me with an intimate community of fellowship in which I have come of age.

In an era when it is under siege by those who have no understanding of it, psychoanalysis, in large part, gave me the conceptual tools that I used to identify and grapple with the issues addressed by this book. At the same time that I was deploying the methods and concepts of the Duluth Domestic Abuse Intervention Project, as well as those of Daniel Sonkin, Del Martin, Lenore Walker (1985), and Edward Gondolf (1985), I was beginning to study psychoanalysis.

Jan Middeldorf taught me how to find the human in the most disturbed and seemingly unreachable patients. Robert Marshall continued that education and provided unbending support and belief in me when in my thinking I dared to push the envelope; no daring consideration has ever been too much for him.

An early draft of this book was read and critiqued by Susan Nimmen-heminda, who helped me along with its birthing.

Faye Peterson showed me how to think thoughts one would tend to shy away from—and how to do so with aplomb and curiosity. Marianne Spitz-form was one of the first to show me the wedding of intellect, dogged pursuit, and serenity.

And Christopher Bollas. Bollas has been a teacher of great dimension and depth, with whom it is my fortune to walk together upon "this good earth of ours." And, lately, James Grotstein has kept me honest and ensured a healthy measure of doubt and rethinking, again and again when need be.

I have been the grateful recipient of the much needed interest in and support of this book by John Michel at Columbia University Press; his warm and always unpretentious way of carrying his considerable force have been a pleasure.

Katharine Turok not only helped me learn how to write better, but she did so in the most affable and intelligent of ways.

INTIMATE VIOLENCE

INTRODUCTION

LEAVING THE ISLAND

On the ferry, on the last morning of summer,
a father at the snack counter deep in the boat
gets breakfast for the others. *Here, let me drink some of*
Mom's coffee, so it won't be so full
for you to carry, he says to his son,
a boy of ten or eleven. The boat
lies lower and lower in the water as the last
cars drive on, it tilts its massive
grey floor like the flat world. Then the
screaming starts, *I carry four things,*
and I only give you one, and you drop it,
what are you, a baby? a high, male
shrieking, and it doesn't stop, *Are you two?*
Are you a baby? I give you one thing,
no one in the room seems to move for a second,
a steaming pool spreading on the floor, little
sea with its own waves, the boy
at the shore of it. *Can't you do anything*
right? Are you two? Are you two?, the piercing
cry of the father. *Go away,*
go up to your mother, get out of here—
he purser swabbing the floor, the boy
not moving from where the first word touched him,
and I could not quite walk past him, I paused
and said *I spilled my coffee on the deck, last trip,*

it happens to us all. He turned to me,
his lips averted so the gums gleamed,
he hissed a guttural hiss, and in
a voice like Gollum's or the Exorcist girl's when she
made that stream of vomit and beamed it
eight feet straight into the minister's mouth
he said *Shut up, shut up, shut up,* as if
protecting his father, peeling from himself
a thin wing of hate, and wrapping
it tightly around father and son, shielding them.
—Sharon Olds (1999)

Upon referral and a medical records assessment of whether to accept Puck into a community residential treatment center, I was impressed by his apparent hunger to find a home, to have an unrequited longing honored. On meeting him for the first time, I was impressed with his warmth and sincerity. But near the end of his "honeymoon" at Constancy House, I was impressed by how determined he was to be ejected from the home, to see himself as victimized, whereas he was actually wreaking a kind of havoc—proving just how similar to his intimidating and abusive stepfather he could be. He became a demanding ogre, an irritable baby in the man-sized body of a fourteen year old. He soon had the staff and fellow residents paralyzed with fear. He was punching holes in walls of the house, intimidating teachers in the public school system, and was going to have to be discharged to a more secure facility if such actions were not reined in quickly: his probation officer, his child protection worker, and the executive director of the organization overseeing the group home collectively would not abide his misdeeds if his caretakers did not appear to have him in hand.

So how could I reach him? What did I know about him that could provide any clues? Not only did Puck never know his father, he did not even know who the man was; his mother refused to tell him, claiming this to be for his own good. For as long as he could remember, his stepfather had been there. Violent incidents with this man—slapping, pushing, punching, and kicking when middle latency rendered lower-order violence inefficacious—were commonplace throughout his life. Both parent and step-parent used drugs addictively, both were in and out of county jails for drug-related and various petty crimes. By the time Puck was eleven years old, he was in his first psychiatric hospital. There he was very violent and had to be physically restrained with a good deal of frequency. Both he and his only sibling were removed from parental care and became wards of the state by the time Puck was twelve. Though his mother had repeatedly and traumatically failed him—she found yelling and humiliation to be ready tools of control that cowed him and left him in angst, he maintained a tremendous allegiance to her, blaming the stepfather for everything.[1] Puck became a street child, a "juvenile delinquent" in many ways (though not psychopathic), an avaricious consumer of pornography, and a regular combatant against authorities.

Against all odds, for the duration of the year he was there, Puck never had to be physically restrained at Constancy House.[2] He developed instead a fierce loyalty to the home and to me, finding comfort and pride in a strong paternal transference. How was this possible? Why was he only very difficult for us rather than impossible and in need of physical restraint? I believe there are many Pucks in the world who are containable when understood and met in ways that honor their maturational needs and when their caregivers can simultaneously stand up to their defensive rage without retaliation in the name of restraint.

How does all of this happen? Furthermore, how can a young man who is sensitive to the subjective ravages of abuse, and who swears that he will never repeat his father's sins, turn right around and do exactly that? What are the means by which we understand such an ironic enigma? What are the means by which we intervene so as not to collude with him in such a repetition?

IN RECENT DECADES society has become more open to an awareness of the disturbing existence, manifestations, and consequences of domestic or intimate violence, especially spouse abuse and child abuse. The historically powerless—wives and children—have been championed to the point that child protective services and battered women's programs have proliferated, with abuse consciousness becoming pervasive in our culture (even if there is much controversy over what to consider abusive). The atrocities that were still commonplace a half-century ago are no longer tacitly condoned. Society now has laws in place—laws that are intelligently evolving—aimed at protection for the powerless and sanctions against the familial abusers of power.

Social thinkers and policy makers have focused, when bringing these matters to society's awareness, on the more extreme forms of abuse. And in spouse abuse, the major focus of this work, the physical ability and impunity of the male "perpetrator," or batterer, to "solve" problems with violence have been highlighted, perhaps of necessity. In the process, however, society has managed to criminalize what is actually a psychopathology, with all the attendant defensive purposes inherent in that term. The problem with such reasoning is parallel to both August Aichhorn's and

Kurt Eissler's decades-old respective addresses of these same errors regarding delinquents. As Aichhorn wrote:

> Whoever wants to work successfully with young delinquents has to be capable of stepping out of his own secure position in the social community, to identify himself with the offender, and thereby to become receptive to and understanding of the intricacies of the delinquent's character structure. . . . If, however, the educator remains reserved and identified with society, and feels protective of the laws the wayward youth is violating, no meaningful contact can be established. Since the wayward youth remains a stranger to him, the educator will unintentionally assume the role of defender of society rather than bend his efforts toward true rehabilitation of the delinquent. . . . The wayward individual experiences these efforts as coercive to make him relinquish his innate personality and so he fights back. When the educator tries to persuade the delinquent gently and benevolently to give up his subjective personality voluntarily, he sees his efforts fail and then he resorts to violence. . . . In the beginning phase of rehabilitation, it matters not how society views the delinquent and to what extent he is considered a disturbing outsider. Of crucial importance is the need to learn how the wayward youth himself experiences society. (1948:229–230)

Puck is exactly the kind of boy Aichhorn had in mind. He clung to his recalcitrant self and was then met with violence in the name of "needing to be restrained."
Eissler proffered that

> delinquency has also been considered a configuration which developed with the ego's conscious cooperation. . . . This view implies the offender's full responsibility for such behavior whereas the individual's responsibility for a neurotic or psychotic symptom has been repudiated by most modern psychiatrists. Indeed, such arguments must be conceded to be correct as long as delinquency is defined from the viewpoint of the jurist or society. (1949:5)

So, if Puck refuses to comply with a dictate of the authorities, he "asks for it. He refuses to obey."
Eissler continues:

> If a child lacks the ability to integrate the behavior pattern necessary for his protection from physical dangers, e.g., if a child persists in reaching towards fire or

in cutting himself with knives, we assume a basic impairment. . . . A person so afflicted might continue to act that way throughout his adulthood . . . and he will never lose the status of a patient deserving medical attention. If, however, a person as a child is deficient in his capacity or ability to integrate the behavior patterns necessary for dealing with values and therefore persists in that delinquency throughout adulthood, he is not granted the status of a patient but the police and the courts are expected to deal with him. Yet there is no theoretical justification for this marked difference in approach towards the two categories of disturbances. (6–7)

Puck returned to his grossly defiant ways after Constancy House. He was repeatedly "warned" of the consequences if he didn't alter his misdeeds. And we know that he eventually ended up fully criminalized, a state prison inmate. The idea that he needed more sophisticated treatment than the more penal version he was receiving was met with either charges that "he knew what he was doing" or, sadly, that the state could not afford to send him to the kind of facilities known for such work.

Aichhorn's and Eissler's considerations appear simple enough, but it is all too clear that we have poorly heeded them. In 1989 I was exposed to Duluth's Domestic Abuse Intervention Project (henceforth referred to simply as Duluth), at the same time that I was invited by a colleague in Missoula, Montana to help him found M.A.N. (Men Advocating Nonviolence), a program for treating male batterers court-ordered to twenty-five hours of domestic violence counseling following convictions for domestic abuse. Duluth, as I understood it, and the domestic violence field across its varied allied professionals (psychotherapists, counselors, shelter workers, victims' advocates, child protection workers, police, prosecution and defense attorneys, presiding judges, and perhaps also state and federal legislators) seemed quite representative of the field at large. With its popularity and contagion, Duluth is typical of contemporary intervention programs. My experience of it and my encounters with a majority of the field's allied professionals have been characterized by the following contradictions.

On the one hand, Duluth provided a deservingly welcome and clear picture of the various manifestations of domestic abuse, as exemplified by that program's (Pence and Paymar 1993) now well-known power and control wheel (appendix, figure 1). The wheel demonstrates with precise clarity how it is that a number of batterer attitudes and actions serve to support batterers "getting their way," controlling their spouses, escalating to or culminating in actual violence when the other strategic mechanisms of the wheel do not bring the desired results. Thus, for example, if emotional or verbal abuse does not bring the other into compliance with their wishes, batterers may resort to physical violence in order to accomplish their purpose. However, more often than not, the emotional or verbal abuse, with its batterer-inherent threat of violence, will suffice to procure the acquiescence sought after.

So let us say that Harvey wants Michelle to no longer voice her displeasure at his drinking for an hour after work each day at the bar. He has heard these complaints before—"She knows he doesn't want to hear that"—so he contemptuously tells her to "shut the fuck up!" She does not. He stands up from the table, violently, knocking his chair over. He yells the louder, hoping this will get her to be silent. She persists. By now, let us say that she too is yelling. They escalate. He pushes her. Perhaps she persists even then. He pushes harder.

Or perhaps Michelle wants to buy a new lamp she saw downtown. Harvey is the "breadwinner" and quick to remind her of it when she broaches the subject of the lamp that she knows he will not want and will consider too expensive. She feels shamed by his implication that she does not pull her weight, inasmuch as she does not earn a paycheck. Maybe this time she is silenced. If she is not silenced the next time such a matter arises, Harvey can "up the ante" by yelling, intimidation.

The wheel also provided an excellent sense of the spouse-foreclosing-and-negating ambience that pervades, more or less overtly, the domestically violent home, even when violence or its antecedents are quite temporally distant. Thus when Michelle feels that she ought to be embarrassed by not bringing home the bacon, she is lost for the moment, unable to imagine the enriching of the home that her aesthetic choice would have provided. Or perhaps she greeted Harvey with an attempted account of how she stood up to an aggressive salesman that day and felt a sense of future possibilities for self-confidence. Harvey's reaction of disinterest or minimization may raise her hackles. He doesn't want to deal with a wife who has too much self-assertion, though (which he probably doesn't exactly realize), and he feels he has to take her down a peg or two. If she confronts him about any aspect of this, he can grow more shaming. If that doesn't rattle her sense of self-agency, he can exert his physicality.

Or Puck! Imagine a big 190-pound raging boy who refuses the mandate of a 110-pound, 24-year-old female staff member. He begins by glaring his refusal. She tries to hold her adult ground, to maintain a sense of her authority. He screams obscenities at her and tells her he'll "kick her fucking ass" if she doesn't get out of his room immediately. She again attempts to be reasonable and elicit his cooperation. He jumps up and slams his fist into the wall, putting a hole in it, and kicks his bed frame, splintering a part of it. Of course, part of his method, even if not consciously, is to put her on notice that he could assault her at any moment.

In this way the wheel provided tools of eminent discernment in therapists' efforts to listen to batterers and to tease out the pervasiveness of the power and control "tactics" (though that term is often a misnomer) from the accounts the men tend to give us when they first arrive for treatment.[3] Puck might have rendered the above story an account of how this "bitch" would absolutely not honor his need for personal space, no matter how hard he tried to convey it to her; he might make quite an impassioned and convincing show of it.

On the other hand, through the five years I conducted groups for adjudicated batterers, and while I discovered the existence of battering in some patients self-referred for other reasons, I struggled with Duluth and other models.[4] I began to build a picture of the insufficiency and persecutory nature of such a partial view, such a victimology approach. Sure, Puck was terribly invasive and intimidating. But the point so easy to miss is that he was often struggling with tremendous psychological beasts within himself that he had no capacity in the moment, if at all, to articulate and attempt to master.

CAVEATS AND DISCLAIMERS

Before proceeding further I want to dispel certain anticipated objections to humanized and interiorized conceptualizations of batterers and their treatment. First of all, I agree with the accuracy of the power and control wheel, as far as it goes, and appreciate its delineation of what occurs in a domestically violent home. This book in no way ignores what Duluth and numerous consciousness-raising additions to the field (especially Walker 1979, 1984) have taught us or the fact that the toll of domestic violence is high, even among less severe cases. Indeed, in no case ought therapists to assume there is no risk of severe battering or even homicide or homicide-suicide occurring in a given couple. In fact, remaining mindful of these possibilities is one of the most difficult aspects of conducting this work. Nor should we ever forget the terror or the traumatic consequences involved when a physically more powerful person assaults or intimidates a vulnerable family member. This should go almost without saying, but it is understandable and legitimate to fear that therapists will empathize with an aggressor in a way that ignores the person's terror-inducing potential or allows the person to mistake the therapist's understanding as condoning the violence. Last, it does not escape me for a moment that, while they constitute a minority, there are indeed a number of very dangerous and psychopathically sadistic men, men who appear to have no care at all for the harm they do their wives in a myriad of ways that Duluth has eluci- dated. This patient population presents us with ironies and paradoxes with which we must labor.

What brought the need for this book to my attention was a confluence of several major concerns. First, I became aware that the characterization of batterers as utilizing power and control mechanisms simply to "get their way" was necessary but insufficient; it progressively occurred to me that much more needed to be said about motivational factors. Why would any- one settle for such an impoverished way of being with a loved other? I also became concerned with what appeared to be an emerging picture of bat- terers in general as the most unfeeling, calloused, self-centered, brutal, and unthinking of domestically violent men. And while I understood the charge of "revictimizing the victim," I was also troubled that we were act- ing and thinking as though, for the clinician treating the batterer, because a woman is battered is all there is of clinical relevance about her It is as though a man who batters a woman has foregone any claim to consider what she has done. "You battered her, so 'fess up, take your medicine, and stop whining!" too often seems to be the message. Ideas like letting the male batterer discuss any transgressive complaints about his wife, or espe- cially the preempted consideration that his wife might herself be utilizing any of the enactments of the power and control wheel, including escalat- ing the violence when less obtrusive interactions were not yielding her de- sired results, were foreclosed by misinvoking the otherwise useful dynam- ics of "colluding with the batterer's defenses" or "revictimizing the victim." There was no consideration given to the possibility that the truth about any given couple might have to be painstakingly searched out on an individual basis, case by case. Clinicians and others were compelled to per- ceive "batterer versus victim" through the adversarial-process lenses of perpetrator-victim/guilty-innocent that the criminal court system is bound by. And, last, the idea for this book began to dawn on me when I started grappling with the crudeness of our confrontive interventions. We were saying things to our batterer patients that were premature at best, relatively untested for accuracy, derived from suppositions I have been discussing, and, most important, unconcerned with the need for a treatment alliance or anything akin to the development of a positive transference. We were saying things to the patient that were more reflections of Duluth or whatever specific model was being relied upon. In this regard, it was as though we needed to know little about the batterer other than the fact that he battered, which alone could tell us how to intervene. Insufficient regard was given to how to help the batterer change. The patient was merely expected to accept the putative wisdom of our viewpoints because they were *our* viewpoints. Therapists (then of usually adjudicated patients) who behave in such a manner are themselves guilty of simplistic explanations of batterers' motives for violence and dominance: "They do it because they can!" Just as we must inquire more deeply about what is driving our batterer patients, I will address what drives therapists to adopt such simplistic admonitions.

Some readers may find me too harsh a critic of the batterer-therapist community. But I include myself in these assessments and, in my view and experience, batterer-therapists are under tremendous pressure both socially and countertransferentially to think and behave in the ways I am enumerating. A great example of these pressures appeared in a February 2, 2001, Associated Press article in the *Bozeman Daily Chronicle*, entitled "Women's Lobby Faults Martz for Comments on Battering" (5). At a public speech of some 650 audience members, Montana's recently elected first female governor, Judy Martz, was reported as saying, "My husband has never battered me, but then again, I've never given him a reason to." In response to subsequent criticism for this remark, seen as justifying battering, Martz's communications director quoted the governor: "Domestic violence and physical abuse are sensitive to me as a woman, as a mother and as governor. Let me leave no doubt that I consider such actions abhorrent and intolerable."

BACK TO BATTERERS

Batterers who did agree that they were behaving poorly with their wives were far too frustrated with that acknowledgment. They were unable to reliably and consistently alter their violent behavior, leaving them with a great deal of shame or guilt, though of course only after the fact. I remember the stress of a number of our court-ordered patients who could not bring our consciousness-raising, cognitive restructuring, or psychoeducational interventions to bear on the powerful inner events that recurringly beset them and drove them anew to domestic violence. While batterers indeed do all the things the power and control wheel points out (though not all batterers do all of them), the wheel either fails to indicate a motive for these actions and attitudes or else lends itself to the idea that the motive is simply one of an uncaring, infantile, and "neanderthalic" core in all batterers. The axiom "They do it because they can" is true as far as it goes, but it leaves unaddressed why anyone would content themselves with such a shallow, unintimate, and unsatisfying mode of life. Why men, or women, resort to battering is one of the main questions to which I hope to bring considerable light.

While the popular batterer treatment models and the "fast-food" psychotherapy mentality that was pervading our country lent themselves well to a confrontational posture of intervention, it paid inadequate attention to the often painstaking and laborious process of establishing strong enough treatment relationships with batterers. Such a posture often even unwittingly attacks batterers with therapists' censuring portraits of them, yielding unfortunate consequences. One such outcome, which may be more frequent than batterer program outcome studies indicate, is that of the *psychotherapeutic conspiracy* (Langs 1982; Scalia 1994), in which therapist and patient unconsciously collude to yield the false but desired belief that their work together has been successful. Another unfortunate consequence is the generation of unresolvable antagonistic postures between patient and therapist,foreclosing transference-countertransference enactments, which of course are not recognized as such, that remain in effect in various manifest forms until the court-mandated hours of counseling have been exhausted. Both outcomes not only yield an obvious disillusionment with the treatment of origin but also preempt the follow-up voluntary treatment that could exist.

At a Duluth workshop I was surprised and disquieted by the presenters' barely concealed disdain for batterers and their attitudes that "these men need to be put in their places" as ways of ostensibly bringing about behavior change. In fact, to my greater surprise, as I moved more into the work, was finding the same attitude in myself. I noticed a certain glee when my colleagues and I "exposed the batterer for who he was," or otherwise "really nailed him!" Of course, this was difficult to notice. How this "identification with the victim" and the often unrecognized defense of "identification with the aggressor" occur in the therapist will also be addressed in the following pages, as I believe this form of resistance is pervasive among batterer-therapists. Utilizing my 1994 paper in a Chicago research project, Betcher and Ball (1997) suggest that at least an awareness of the concepts and dynamic principles of identification with the aggressor (as well as projective identification, which I will take up later) are prerequisites to successful treatment outcome with batterers.

Whether or not one agrees with this suggestion, if one grants it as a theoretical possibility, Betcher and Ball's research results are ominous: in their survey of twenty batterer-therapists of varying theoretical orientations, they found that only four were able to define those terms. I will define and exemplify them in the body of this book. But for now I will suggest that this major defense so typically deployed by the batterer is, ironically, often parlayed against him under the guise of treatment.

There is an ironically existing, implied threat that certain clinical or theoretical positions in this field are apostatic, heretical, and misguided. Ironic because such psychic heavy-handedness is indeed part of the legitimate lament about the self- and other-foreclosing postures of the batterer. The batterer epitomizes attacks upon psychic interiority. That is, in their misguided efforts to protect themselves against intolerable experiences within, batterers repudiate messages from inside themselves, and corroborating suggestions from their spouses, that their struggles have something to do with their internal, psychic construction. The very idea is attacked. And when the idea's messenger has been the spouse, and if she or he suggests it too strongly or at too inopportune a moment, the spouse may be physically attacked. Of course, the intervention community has rejected the idea of considering psychic interiority. It does this not only by denying the need for any real depth-oriented treatment of batterers, or by failing to see that the batterer ought to be understood as a patient rather than a criminal, but, more insidiously, by failing to examine its own interior with a psychoanalytic lens. Unfortunately, we must see these foreclosures by the domestic violence intervention field as not endemic to it but rather as epidemic. Our culture is rife with it.

American Psychologist (1993, 1999) has issued volumes with major parts of each devoted to its own rendering of what is happening in the domestic violence field; these volumes pronounce, with what I find a disturbing and growth-negating finality, the advances in the field, "advances" that are blind to interior considerations. Yet in negating the interior of the batterer one is simultaneously negating, doing violence to, one's own interior, one's own integrity. Shunning the batterer and the relevance of his psychic life finds the transgressor guilty of too many of the laments he rightly makes regarding the batterer. Even Celani (1994), who gives us a rendering of an object relations grasp of battered women and batterers, unfortunately disavows the very possibility of a depth-oriented treatment of batterers, believing them untreatable and considering it one of his goals of treating battered women to eventually have them "understand" that they must leave their men if they are to have lives free of spousal oppression. And even Dutton, who has borrowed from his psychoanalytic neighbors in a fine effort to humanize the treatment of batterers, neglects to address the countertransference disruptions in the therapist, i.e., neglects the interior of the therapist in this work. Fortunately, though, he is wise enough to say that after his recommended cognitive therapy the batterer would ideally have access to long-term, depth-oriented treatment. It is to this longer-term treatment that I will address myself.

In my nascent efforts to treat some batterers in a long-term depth-oriented manner, with the help of a "tripartite psychoanalytic training" (with its components of didactic, supervisory, and personal analytic treatment), and as my struggles with domestic violence work in general began to bear fruit, a number of key concerns began to crystallize. They will form the outline of this book. Relevant psychoanalytic concepts and terminology are explored within the framework of their elucidation of domestic violence. These ideas are clearly compatible with those of the field, but only with the following provisos: 1. if the therapist struggles sufficiently with difficult ambiguities that will be encountered throughout the work; only 2. if the therapist sufficiently overcomes the urge to yield to his or her wish for facile and impulsive case conceptualizations, an urge that can become quite powerful in these cases; and only 3. if the analyst resists the urge to carte-blanche declare these patients "unanalyzable" and struggles instead with his or her own resistances to treating them.

Conversely, I would suggest to the psychoanalytic community not only 1. that these patients are often enough good candidates for contemporary psychoanalytic treatment, when it is equipped to handle preverbal and narcissistic concerns, but also 2. that there may be more batterers in psychoanalytic caseloads than recognized, and 3. that treating batterers psychoanalytically may strengthen psychoanalysis in general while simultaneously offering our services in an arena where they seldom find room but are sorely needed. My formal psychoanalytic training took some pains to include in our studies the exigencies and vicissitudes of well-concealed but nonetheless unneutralized aggression, often in highly functioning patients;

this training has been invaluable. The tripartite training model of psychoanalysis is rigorous but irreplaceable—unsubstitutable, in my opinion. Conversely, again, there is a stark dearth of psychoanalytic literature on batterers, where this very type of patient is possibly often shunned. As a fellow psychoanalytic candidate once put it when I mentioned something about a batterer in a class, "Oh, no! We're not gonna talk about batterers, are we?!" Again, would I be noticing a relative preponderance of domestic violence—whether one was hitting or being hit—in my patients' histories were it not for programs like Duluth and M.A.N., writers like Lenore Walker or Daniel Sonkin?

Divided into three parts, *Intimate Violence* deals first with some psychoanalytic contributions to the understanding of the inner mechanisms of the batterer's violence, a psychic interior of it. Part 2 analyzes our society's rather persecutory depictions and uses of the concepts of abuse and batterer, along with our general ideas about victims, and suggests alternative views and renderings. Part 3 addresses treatment considerations that I believe to be indispensible if we wish to effect permanent, deep, and thoroughgoing changes in batterers.

The first part, "Understanding the Batterer," consists of three chapters, beginning with "Affect Regulation and Narcissistic Equilibrium," which explores the individual's ability to maintain sufficient mastery or dominance of his emotional states. In batterings, we see intolerable and overwhelming emotional states that are not contained or managed—arguably, by either party; instead they may be dammed up until the retaining wall collapses, is burst. Narcissistic equilibrium, i.e., the maintenance of a sufficiently good feeling about and good estimation of oneself and one's place in the world, is also severely and dangerously disrupted. Both spouses in one young couple began treatment with me following their expectation that they would both soon be court-ordered to treatment. In expressing her grave frustration with the legal system's interactions with her and her husband, the wife said, "Why do they treat us like criminals, like we did this on purpose or something, when it's just that we can't handle our feelings sometimes?!" The reader may recognize how uncannily she echoes Eissler. We will look at how the patient fails to exercise, summon, or recognize responsibility for these ego functions and the interpersonal and intrapsychic consequences of the failures and functions this woman spoke of. We will notice how it is that the patient may be aware at one point that these functions are rightly to be seen as originating internally, while being at other times wholly unable to summon that knowledge. The ideas of narcissistic character pathology inherent in battering will be discussed, also considering those batterers who are more accurately understood as "pseudonarcissistic psychoneurotics," much more highly structured individuals who nonetheless regress into narcissistic rage in quite specific situations (Kohut 1972; Scalia 1994, 1998). Spotnitz's (1976, 1985) "narcissistic defense," in which the subject maintains a self-foreclosing, and in our case other-foreclosing, warding off of imminently threatening early trauma, will also be examined. In order to prevent being overwhelmed by early cumulative traumata reactivated with a spouse, the batterer transfers over the usual self-attack inherent in the narcissistic defense to assaults on his spouse.

A look at several analysts' work, chapter 2, "The Experience of Self and Other," incorporates the ideas of Margaret Mahler et al., Daniel Stern, and Christopher Bollas. Mahler, Pine, and Bergman's (1975) now classic work is reviewed, especially as it relates to the batterer's psychic structure, typical or most relied upon defense mechanisms, and, especially, impairments in the capacity to experience the other appreciatively and empathically. Daniel Stern's later work, which from my perspective is a natural segue to Mahler's, in its pertinence to battering provides a more experience-near sense of the patient's inner events, speaks directly to the disequilibratory component of my theory of batterer breakdown, and provides another angle from which to view the readily embraceable humanity of the batterer than we are accustomed to hearing about. Christopher Bollas's (1987) transformational object, unthought known, and idiom will also figure in my considerations.

Chapter 3, "Identification with the Aggressor," deals with a battering-ubiquitous defense mechanism, first named, formulated, and expounded by Sandor Ferenczi (1933) and further elaborated by Anna Freud (1936). When I first began work with batterers, I was surprised by the very high percentage of court-ordered cases in which the batterer would report an incident of egregious abuse by one or both parents but justify it, often saying things like, "I deserved it, I was being a little brat," or else, "I'm glad they did it, or how else would I ever have learned?" Later, of course, the subject demonstrated some of that same abusiveness and likewise saw it as acceptable behavior on his part. When the manner in which this justification of his original tormentor's abuse of him is interpreted, and when his subsequent identification with that abusive aspect of his parent(s) becomes clear, as a way in which the little child protected himself from intolerable conscious experiences, considerable progress is made toward understanding the dynamics of intimate violence.

Part 2, "The Politics of the Batterer Treatment Movement," addresses certain salient miscarriages of justice and attendant clinical distortions I have found to permeate the field. It also offers some conceptual modifications helpful in remedying these errors. Chapter 4, "Political Versus Clinical Determinations of Abuse and Other Associations" postulates intrapsychic and intersubjective events that are suggested as necessary considerations in our designations of abuse, as opposed to limiting ourselves to more overtly observable interpersonal and behavioral data. Topics such as the legal system's/battered women's movement's/therapists' often false dichotomizations of batterer-versus-victim, the inherent vilification of the batterer, and the foreclosed consideration of what constitutes a battering patient make up chapter 5, "Our Unwitting Persecution of the Batterer and Other Facile Conveniences." The relatively intractable and pervasive, even if decried and repudiated, persecutory nature of group life is considered as another driving force.

"Treatment," the last major part of the book, begins with chapter 6's look at "Countertransference," our reactions to the patient's uses of and relation to us, i.e., our relation to the transference. The chapter articulates and examines some of the titanic tasks the therapist must successfully negotiate, unbeknownst to patients, if he or she is to aid the batterer into a realm of sufficient observing ego and contemplation of self and other.

Chapter 7, "Transference," explores the need for patients to experience us as people who have something of importance to offer them and gives a nascent exploration of how different patients will require different ministrations. For example, clinicians must differentiate between a man who is already troubled by his abusive behavior and wishes to change it and a man who thinks there is absolutely nothing wrong with what he does. How we proceed according to this division ought to be as different as night and day, in some ways, though clearly determined by a multitude of further considerations as well.

In chapter 8, "Joining Techniques," we consider how, with such an individual, we would not or ought not to demand greater ability for accurate self examination (i.e., observing ego) than he or she is capable of; to do so only degenerates potentially meaningful access to patients. We should instead pay credence to the prominence of the "afflicted ego" (Geltner 1995) and attempt to generate interventions that would not require a subjects' cognizance of what we were doing for the sake of their psychological development. In "Psychoanalysis and Violence," Phyllis Meadow stated:

> We have learned techniques for reducing the pressure for discharge by reinforcing infantile defenses as in the joining techniques developed by Spotnitz. . . . We have become more expert in bringing defenses into focus, managing them until they are outgrown, rather than analyzing them. . . . One of the principles that we sometimes forget is that analyzing resistances, that is, interpreting them to the patient, may not resolve them. It may lead to the patient bottling them up. . . . When shut up, they turn to destructive acts. (1997:13)

We enact the function here of an "auxiliary ego," doing for patients both what they cannot do intrapsychically and what they don't even realize needs doing. These are methods of "emotional communication" as opposed to something more in the nature of cognitive communication, such as confrontation, interpretation, consciousness-raising techniques, or cognitive restructuring techniques, though any of these may sometimes properly overlap more emotional-communicative expressions.

Chapter 9, "Working Through: A Synthesis" places the concepts of preceding chapters into an experience-near sense, and several cases from previous chapters are followed up and elaborated.

PART 1
UNDERSTANDING THE BATTERER

CHAPTER ONE

AFFECT REGULATION
AND NARCISSISTIC EQUILIBRIUM

Childhood love is boundless, it demands exclusive possession,
it is not content with less than all.
—Sigmund Freud (1931)

Rycroft defines affect as a "general term for feelings and emotions" (1968:3). And it is the ego that is responsible for the regulation and management of affect. Freud said of the ego that it "presents what may be called reason and common sense, in contrast to the id, which contains the passions. . . . In its relation to the id it is like a man on horseback, who has to hold in check the superior strength of the horse" (1923:25). This metaphor represents the greater strength of the batterer's id, specifically his affects during battering, which become uncontainable.

An individual whose affect regulation is impaired only in circumscribed situations, to a lesser rather than greater degree, will present a far different general clinical picture, and specific battering picture, than the person who batters in any number of circumstances and whose tolerance of difficult emotion is severely restricted. The latter will tend toward violence more frequently, with less external provocation and greater physical severity.

Already weaving through these ego-psychological considerations are the self-psychological conceptualizations of narcissistic equilibrium/disequilibrium and narcissistic rage. Ernest Wolf defines narcissistic rage as "a form of potentially violent aggression that aims to destroy an offending selfobject [to be defined below] when this selfobject is experienced as threatening the continued cohesion or existence of the self, particularly when this threat to the self takes the form of imposing helplessness on the self" (1988:000). A selfobject (Kohut 1984) would be that experience, often represented by a significant other (or "object," when the object is a person), to which the self attaches in a manner that allows it a good-enough estimation of itself and a sufficient sense of self-cohesion.

Matt was seeing me in couples therapy when he suddenly jumped out of his seat, fist reared back, threatening to hit me. He had no real idea of what had just set him off. He even looked rather confused as he stood there, as though he were wondering to himself, "How the hell did I get HERE, standing over this guy like this?" I discuss this incident and its resolution at greater length, so will say only that I had been in dialogue with his wife when suddenly he popped! Something in the way he feels secure had been threatened. I was the cause of this threat and he had to stop it, without deliberation.

Or Puck. Puck became enraged when, in the group home, he was not allowed to keep a padlock on his bedroom door. This locked space seemed to represent to him a nurturing darkness, a space in which he could feel held in safety, cohered. When his vocal intimidation did not win him his way, he began to punch holes in the walls of the house, first outside the staff office, then in his room.[1] The loss of this space, which seemed to serve a selfobject function, was more than he could bear.[2]

Here, Wolf may be helpful: a selfobject is "the *subjective* aspect of a self-sustaining function performed by a relationship of self to objects who by their presence or activity evoke and maintain the self and the experience of selfhood" (1988:184). In an earlier work on batterers, I quoted Wolf in a passage that should be disturbingly familiar to those who work with domestic violence. Then, as I do again now, I prefaced his words with "In the author's experience, batterers are typically [though not always] men with significant characterological disturbance, narcissistically wounded men who experienced harsh [and unintegratable/unprocessable] treatment early in life. Perhaps ironically, their experience with their victims is often one of helplessness and narcissistic vulnerability" (Scalia 1994:549). I follow this passage with Wolf's "There is hardly a more frightening situation than the threat of helplessness. Individuals respond to this threat with narcissistic rage—a self's unlimited rage that aims to destroy the origin of the threat to itself. Homicide and suicide are the not uncommon outcomes when there seems to exist no other action to do away with the experience of helplessness" (49). Puck did not go so far as that, but it was easy to see how he could have escalated had we not understood the threat he felt.

While there are other motives for domestic homicides, suicides, and homicide-suicides, this narcissistically defended motive is, I suggest, by far the most common. When batterers are demonized, vilified, or dehumanized, we are a far cry indeed from being able to integrate such a point of view into our overall picture of them. Yet even the batterer's male-apologist-ascribed motive to control his spouse must often be understood as secondary to a struggle for self-cohesion, primarily motivated by an immediate need to end overwhelming self-pathology suffering, to force the environment into providing comfort and sustenance.

Imagine an obsessive-compulsive man, in disagreement with his wife, who is an hysteric. He is telling her about a struggle he had earlier that day, how he had behaved with a customer who he felt was trying to take advantage of him. In his view of things, he had overcome his usual tendency to be easily pushed around, to acquiesce to demanding others. He is proud of how he asserted himself and was not a milquetoast. Yet, she hears his story as an incident of embarrassment, interprets his behavior as boorish and tells him so. He is wounded, say narcissistically injured. She may be insulting him out of her own sense of having felt degraded or narcissistically injured, by imagining a social encounter with her husband's customer. In response to her insult, imagine that he feels impelled to extract an apology from her. Unless he derives support from her, he is unable to sustain a good self-estimation. She responds to his entreaty—or demand—with further indignation and degradation of him. Matters escalate.

Battering may be seen as a defense against the threat of narcissistic disequilibrium. It also goes hand in hand with the ego-defense of "identification with the aggressor," which will be explored in chapter 3. Battering occurs when the subject finds no alternative to restoring a sufficient sense of narcissistic equilibrium, sufficient freedom from perceived environmental *impingements*, to the extent that the subject may maintain a sense of *going-on-being* (Winnicott 1965), a sense that he will survive. Battering is also a defense against what Winnicott (1962) called *unthinkable anxiety*—or the psychotic anxiety of "going to pieces"; indeed, some batterers experience "flying apart/exploding apart (from within)," only a slight modification of Winnicott's term. Thus, if we think of battering as a defense against affect deregulation, or narcissistic disequilibrium, we need to understand the implicit, intrapsychic, intervening variable(s) between them. Identification with the aggressor will be shown to be one of these variables, and in fact a necessary one.

SOURCES OF AFFECT DISREGULATION/NARCISSISTIC DISEQUILIBRIUM AND THE PATHOGNOMONIC BATTERER DEFENSES AGAINST THEM

How is it that our obsessive patient mentioned above is not able to manage being insulted without experiencing a crisis of self-cohesion? These impaired ego functions in the batterer are a product of developmental goings astray whose origins or foundational roots predate the oedipal period of development. Without going into any explication of the oedipal period, it might simply be said that the batterer lacks an adequate observing ego. It is during preoedipal development that the groundwork for the establishment of the observing ego occurs. The separation-individuation stage of development is particularly pertinent here and will be returned to in chapter 2. But for now, around issues pursuant to battering, around issues pursuant to affect regulation and narcissistic equilibrium, the batterer is more or less unable to observe (before, during, or after battering) his own responsibility for his violence.

There is a noteworthy exception to the statement I have made, one that has to do with the type of patient that Kohut (1972) called a *pseudonarcissistic psychoneurotic*; this is a point of significant clinical and social relevance and will be taken up separately. But the batterer we are most familiar with, the type that we villainize, is disturbed in his capacity to fully contemplate that it is he who "did the deed." He certainly knows that he physically strikes out, but he does not locate the responsibility for his misbehavior squarely within himself. Even among batterers who appear to understand the actual chain of events, careful idiographic clinical study must be made, as they may not have this knowledge deeply integrated. Or, if they do, they will be unable to maintain it in certain stressful situations (this would be our *pseudonarcissist*) and will resort to the following character-defensive posture so as to justify their renewed use of battering when they become once more unable to regulate their own affect or maintain their own narcissistic equilibrium.

It is of the utmost importance to emphasize that when an individual batters to regulate his overwhelming affect, he is not intending to victimize anyone, at least not consciously and at least not as a primary action. The motive to batter is always secondary to the primary motive of protecting the inner self. The individual victim is not the actual other but an internal "object" threatening the self. That this internal object is externalized in order for battering to occur is merely a function of the subject's inability in the moment to recognize any projective occurrence taking place within him.

At that point, obviously, there is a failed empathic function, which will also be separately taken up in chapter 2. But, for now, something must be said about "character defenses" (Fenichel 1945), for it is character defenses that give the batterer his stated rationales, justifications, rationalizations for why he batters.

In discussing reactive character traits, Fenichel explained how habitual defensive attitudes are used to protect the subject against threatening stimulation, be it external or internal, instinctual or emotional. These are character defenses. Blaming others is a universal character defense of batterers.

In the current political-psychological climate with regard to domestic violence, it needs to be stated that this defense operates whether or not the subject is correct in his assessment that his other has mistreated him in some fashion.[3] Even when the other has been defensively or egocentrically wounding toward the subject, that subject still relies upon blame of the object for his own failure to manage his internal responses, for his failure to contain what is occurring within him. Helping the batterer sort out objective disappointments or grievances—that is, helping him sort out when his spouse has behaved hurtfully toward him—from those events in which he has erroneous expectations and perceptions of her should hardly be understood as "colluding with the batterer." Yet it is misconstrued in just this way by many individuals and by many guiding principles within the domestic violence field. The fear of acknowledging legitimate batterer grievances against his spouse is that he will feel more justified in blaming her for his behavior, more justified in the battering itself or in its precursors and sequelae. In point of fact, however, with each improvement of the subject's observing ego, which such differentiation affords, comes concomitant ego strengthenings of various types, all of which ameliorate his need for the defense of battering and for character defenses in general.

One of these ego functions, aimed at regulating affect, is emotional insulation. Freud (1920:27) spoke of a "protective shield," presaging Spotnitz's (1987 [1976]) development of the concepts of stimulus barrier and emotional insulation. Spotnitz describes intrauterine life as the beginning of the development of a stimulus barrier and the mother's body as the prototype of this barrier, as it "provides a shock-free atmosphere . . . from the excessive impact of the surrounding organs—the impinging environment" (122). After birth, the mother, usually the primary caregiver, continues to perform her insulative role; but she shifts from the involuntary biological operations of the gestation period to voluntary activity that will facilitate (the infant's) adjustment and growth in a more rigorous environment. By meeting the infant's maturational needs through the proper balance of gratification and frustration, she helps to prepare his body and mind to take over the task of insulating himself.

Spotnitz discusses the normal development of the stimulus barrier and emotional insulation, pointing out that during the first few years of life nervous tissue is being sheathed in myelin, its own insulating substance.[4] It may be that deficits in emotional stimulation will have to be activated in the transference-countertransference matrix (Marshall and Marshall 1988), with outcomes quite different from the psychopathogenic or neuropathogenic ones. If this happens time after time, might neurological change occur alongside the psychostructural? This is a different matter, and will be dealt with in part 3.

After a review of Freud's (1950; released in 1950, though actually written a half-century earlier) "Project for a Scientific Psychology" and the studies of Wilder Penfeld and his associates at the Montreal Neurological Institute, Spotnitz (1987) maintains:

> The findings just reviewed shed some light on what transpires in a patient's nervous system during the psychotherapeutic process. They also suggest that, when we ask him to cooperate in the two-fold task of developing healthful forms of insulation and the appropriate verbal discharge patterns he needs, we are actually making enormous demands on the patient. These demands involve the reorganization and reintegration of his nervous system.
>
> Any kind of talking won't do this job. The exceedingly intricate neurophysiological mechanisms involved in talking are utilized to secure the release into language of certain feelings that were associated with highly charged emotional experiences. The patient must verbalize the destructive impulses that he has been holding in check through pathological forms of insulation. If he does not possess sufficient patterns for verbal discharge, he has to be assisted in developing additional patterns. (128)

We may actually be asking batterers to undergo a process such that neurophysiological change must occur concomitantly with psychostructural alteration. Or, if real psychostructural change is going to occur in the batterer, does neurophysiological change inevitably occur with it? Must there be reroutings in the brain, requiring great effort, in order for real psychostructural change to occur in the batterer?

Similarly, Bollas (1987) speaks of language in psychoanalysis as having a transformational function; but implicit in this concept is the notion that we are dealing with deeply rooted and hitherto unthought but known, and deeply influential, defining, and orienting subjective experiences. Inherent in both theoreticians' concepts is the idea that the primary and deepest motivational factors must become activated and elucidated in the treatment. Overlaying these phenomena with interventions that do not reach them, that do not attempt to articulate and transform them, is doomed to fail.

So often treatment for batterers consists of inculcating them in the interpersonal politics of the power and control wheel, or some other consciousness-raising schema. Other treatments try to provide batterers with techniques for calming down when their anger begins to mount. These are ideas that are easily conveyed in short periods of time but that do not reach very far inside the batterer's experience. They are topical and universally applied. They have no chance of dealing with something as big as psychic structures that appear to have organic substrates or actual organic concomitants.

An example may help to carry my point. A twelve-year-old boy has been having temper tantrums all his life. He has felt deeply violated over and over, beginning when his parents could not calm him as an infant and they grew very frustrated, felt persecuted by him, and acted to stop what were to them impingements on their *going-on-being*. His mother would grow cold and remote; his father would become rough with him, convey a bit of a threat. This began in infancy when he cried past the parents' comfort zones. As he got a little older, the nature of the threats changed, but the frustration was a familiar one. He felt a deep injustice that became almost his closest companion (Bollas's *conservative object* [1987]). In the mind or the brain of the batterer, one can metaphorically imagine deep channels carrying affective and interpersonal experience, channels worn ever deeper over time, with higher canyon walls ever building. These channels carry *the passion and pathos of ill-treatment* and the helpless fight against it. When the forces that built this channel system change, the courses will not change easily with them. They are channelized, and the water doesn't flow easily out of them.

The batterer's defensive employments reveal a very rigid ego attitude, one of blaming the spouse or children for any of the batterer's violence. When the patient "can't stand the heat in the kitchen," when the interpersonal environment overstimulates or overwhelms him, and when he strikes out in abusive ways, *he does not then believe that he is misbehaving. At that moment there is no observing ego in operation to decide, selfishly, that he would rather be abusive than struggle with his inner experiences. Instead he experiences himself, subjectively, in an emergency situation; he automatically and nonself-reflectively strikes out, for the purpose of restoring inner calm and self-cohesion.*

Most unfortunately, and to the chagrin of psychotherapists (though most of us seem to defend against this painful knowledge), these functions are *not* within the conscious view of the subject. Even those individuals who express genuine remorse for their actions did not have access to that part of themselves when battering.

Wish all we will that this were not so, and try all we might to deploy various cognitively based interventions in the absence of attending to these serious ego and character deviations, unless we allow ourselves, consistently, the awareness of these subjects' salient character incapacities we are at a complete loss in any effort to be helpful. When the subject cannot regulate his affective state or his narcissistic equilibrium, he cannot contemplate these ego deficits. He cannot think about the need for a *time-out*. He is overwhelmed not only by the moment but by his more or less disavowed pathogenic history.

All ego- and self-impinging experiences that forestalled his developing sufficient and mature ego functioning seem violently drawn to his immediate subjective experience like steel to a powerful magnet, and he is overwhelmed by subjective experiences of helplessness now and then. Whatever ego he may ordinarily have available to him is momentarily *obliterated*.

In this vein, I recall a poignant incident with Jacques, a proud and virile teen who was in my care at a community residential treatment center that I directed in Bozeman. Jacques, whom I had then seen for some three hundred hours of individual psychoanalytic work, "snapped" when staff members attempted to routinely respond to a minor house infraction. He had endured incredible privation and abuse in the home of his mother and stepfather, having been finally and permanently removed from their care when the stepfather literally stabbed him in the back, puncturing a lung and nearly killing him. I will have more to say about this case in part 3, but for now it need only be understood that, by the time of the incident under consideration, he had developed a strong idealizing transference to me; he thought the world of me—as in fact he still does, in a more realistic way—and "in his right mind" would never have done anything to hurt me.

When I arrived on the scene, having been summoned by my alarm at the explosion I was hearing a couple of rooms away, Jacques had the whole house held in the grip of his thundering rage. Imagining that his transference would allow me to intervene with relative ease, which turned out to be true as far as it goes, the intensity of being in his immediate proximity, and his considerable physical prowess, more than a little changed my point of view. All of his potent and facilitating transference to me barely saved the day. He yelled at me, screaming "in my face" in a quite threatening way. I was afraid he would become physically violent. Most clearly, that part of him which, even at that point in his treatment and personal development (which is considerably more advanced now), would ordinarily have held in check any assault upon me was *obliterated* in those inundating moments, only to be recovered shortly thereafter, finding him deeply distressed at having struck out so harshly at me. During the crucible of the incident I was not my *self* for him—I was not the object he'd known for so long as transformational. I was the representation of all that had oppressed and, indeed, tried to actually *obliterate* him. Had he hit *me*, it would not have been me he was hitting.

Contrarily, when the subject, after battering, does not believe that he has misbehaved, we are dealing with more pervasive defenses against remembering and articulating pathogenic, developmentally salient experiences of helplessness at the hands of his own early caregivers. In treatment, we must be able to ultimately reactivate these pathogenic experiences, as the patient's neurological and psychostructural equipment becomes capable (each such event with a positive transference-countertransference outcome making him further capable), such that these defenses can gradually lose their death-grip on the ego. To do so will require tremendous strengths and endurances by the therapist, a great deal more than the mere twenty-five to fifty court-mandated hours we currently see, and much more than only cognitively based interventions. For example, we must cognize—as important information, without succumbing to the wish to enact—our registrations of impulses to be rid of some of these patients. As we are asking a great deal of them, it would behoove us to ask as much of ourselves, and to look more deeply at just what we are asking.

Terry and Alice come easily to mind. Against financial and sociocultural odds, this young couple stayed in treatment with me for many months beyond the court mandate. Terry would often make much ado about nothing, complaining about Alice. Many hours were consumed by his empty swagger before I could finally see, through the fog, a real person worth knowing. Through those hours I often was either very bored or impatient with him. Meaningful engagement was not possible, and I had to bide my time. The temptation to act out scornfully toward him was great, an acting out I knew would rid me of him. Finally there emerged something of an arrested, cute little boy who wanted to be admired, much like Terry's own son, who was frequently in sessions and who Terry often managed to blow off, unawares, in ways we can easily imagine he also endured repeatedly. I came to see his unconscious scorn for his son's longing and vulnerability, a scorn that was part of his identification with his own father. In the countertransference I felt the same scorn for Terry (Racker's *concordant and complementary identifications* [1968]).

It was noteworthy that he consciously esteemed this boy, but it was not quite the boy he esteemed but rather his idea of him, a projective identification. The real son received little benevolence because of it. Terry was able to have this son—himself really—in an imaginary world, while investing very little care in his actual son.

THE PSEUDONARCISSISTIC PSYCHONEUROTIC

Heinz Kohut (1972) pointed out that there are individuals who seem narcissistically disturbed but, on close analytic relating, reveal themselves to possess relatively solid ego structures and are basically neurotically organized. Upon a certain amount of distress the pseudonarcissistic neurotic will momentarily deteriorate into a narcissistic crisis, then being unable to utilize typical ego strengths and attributes.

Thus, for example, a batterer may typically have an empathic connection to their spouse, but under certain stress, or otherwise altered affect, will momentarily lose that capacity for empathy. It is merely unavailable; it is not capriciously and conveniently abrogated for the sake of ease. In point of fact, it is precisely this batterer who will suffer pangs of regret for violent and denigrating actions. How many of the batterers who are conceptualized in the cycle of violence as remorseful after battering fall into this category?

While I imagine this type is the exception, I do not know that, and it is probably the case that it can only be determined were there to be a deepgoing psychotherapy, and if the therapist were to have the question answered spontaneously in the natural course of treatment. As we have relatively few documented cases of psychoanalytic treatment of batterers, we simply have no data base upon which to proceed to anything other than a priori hypotheses.

Pablo, a man ordinarily in distress, worried a lot about his wife's financial inadequacies. He was usually able to separate his wife's true inability to suddenly make any financial contribution to a strapped family budget, on the one hand, and his practically unrelenting anxiety about money, on the other.

At times, though, he could not hold this differentiation, would be unable to maintain his usual compassion for her quite distressing plight, and could then only experience her as a grave source of privation. At these times he could easily become intensely berating of her and very threatening. Were we to see him as narcissistically disturbed, and in need of a "narcissistic transference," a lot of time could be wasted. Recognizing his tenuous capacity for whole object relations, he could be helped to foster an inquiring attitude about his oscillations and begin to get on with the program.

Winnicott, pursuant to the need for regression to dependence in the transference, imagined patients within three categories of intervention need. There are, first, patients capable of whole object relations, or, as Winnicott put it, those "who operate as whole persons. . . . The technique for the treatment of these patients belongs to psycho-analysis as it developed in the hands of Freud at the beginning of the century."

Then *secondly* there come the patients in whom the wholeness of the personality only just begins to be something that can be taken for granted; in fact one can say that analysis has to do with the first events that belong to and inherently and immediately follow not only the achievement of wholeness but also the coming together of love and hate and also the dawning recognition of dependence. This is the analysis of the stage of concern, or of what has come to be known as the "depressive position." These patients require the analysis of mood. The technique for this work is not different from that needed by patients in the first category; nevertheless some management problems do arise on account of the increased range of clinical material tackled. (279)

In Winnicott's third group we find many batterer cases.

In the *third* grouping I place all those patients whose analyses must deal with the early stages of emotional development before and up to the establishment of the personality as an entity. . . . The personal structure is not yet securely founded. In regard to this third grouping, the accent is more surely on management, and sometimes over long periods with these patients ordinary analytic work has to be in abeyance, management being the whole thing. (279)

Jacques and Puck were clearly in this third realm, as will become clear later on when the early parts of their treatments are discussed. They very much required the establishment of the kind of narcissistic transference that Aichhorn, Spotnitz, and Kohut have all spoken of. And indeed, for quite some time, management was everything.

However, Pablo was in the second category. Thus, he did not require a narcissistic transference proper. He was not fundamentally narcissistically disturbed. But he did need aspects of such care. I think we are better equipped to give the Pablos of the world what they need if we think in Winnicott's terms about them: that they are in need of both ordinary analytic work *and* a regression to dependence, the latter of which can happen within the former, that is, within the confines of the free associative process, so long as the analyst is guided in his technique and sensibilities by the factor of dependency regression.

For the pseudonarcissistic patient, if we remain too long in the error of "providing" a narcissistic transference, eventually—though this may take some time as the psuedonarcissist will enjoy elements of it—we will lose them to boredom and their correct assumption that nothing of curative merit is occurring in the analysis.

Per contra, they may be treated by ordinary work and give us the illusion of a progress that is based on a false self compliance. The dependency regressive work must also occur.

A BRIEF NOTE ON DIAGNOSIS

While the DSM (*Diagnostic and Statistical Manual of Mental Disorders*) allows us such diagnostic terms as *intermittent explosive disorder* for the batterer, it is necessary to recognize that DSM offers descriptive diagnostic entities without addressing anything of underlying and conceptually integrating psychostructural considerations. Before DSM-III there was a psychoanalytic underpinning to the manual; obviously this underpinning is what I am relying upon. When we do so, it is easy to recognize that "intermittent explosive disorders," for example, or batterers, do not fit any single diagnostic category. In fact, clinical observation makes it obvious that batterers occupy a vast array of such categories, from the neurotic, to the character disordered, to the perverse, to the psychotic. In this light it is important to recognize that "batterer" is not a diagnosis at all but rather a symptom across diagnoses, having different functions within their varying diagnostic categories.

THE CONCEPTS UNITED

Thus far we have treated a number of concepts that may now be conceptually unified so as to give us a cohesive picture of what it is the batterer is unconsciously defending against as well as this chapter's contribution to why he is so defending. We have stated that the subject cannot tolerate certain of his emotional experiences, cannot "keep a handle on" them, and that he cannot consistently maintain a good-enough inner estimation of himself and his worthiness. These are our concepts of affect deregulation and narcissistic disequilibrium.

We have also looked at the related concepts of the stimulus barrier and of emotional insulation. The batterer has psychostructural and related neurophysiological impairments, both being psychologically reparable, that prevent him from sufficiently regulating his affective states (as well as his narcissistic equilibrium). The stimulus barrier, which allows for emotional insulation, becomes the vehicle or the *neuropsychological structure* that carries the immediate burden of affect regulation.

Character defenses, then, enter our conceptual picture in the following way. When any of these functions becomes inoperative, and battering ensues, we understand that the subject is blaming the other for their own failure in self-regulation. Blaming is a character defense that protects subjects from conscious experience of their inadequacies and helplessness. Imagining the source of their intolerable experience to be their spouses (or children, as the case may be), these become the recipients of battering.

The intervening variable of "identification with the aggressor" is the psychodynamic vehicle that allows for the character-defensive operation. Identification with the aggressor is itself, or ought to be, a major topic of consideration in battering and will be dealt with separately in chapter 3.

INTERNAL MOTIVATIONAL DIALOGUE

As the subject is approaching a battering situation, his inner experience, were he able to describe it, would be something like the following. *"Ah!! I cannot stand it! I am being made to feel like total shit. It is completely unbearable! I am going to fly apart at the seams, explode, become totally obliterated!"* He clearly feels that his subjective experience is "being done to him" in the present. He has no sense of any pathogenic developmental roots, or of anything else theoretically causal. Instead, it is as though an explosive device is about to literally rupture his psyche, his entire self, his whole being, and he must avert disaster. For the subject, it must be understood that this is a distinct survival emergency.

Spotnitz (1987) has introduced the concept of the narcissistic defense as a self-attack designed to protect an image of a good internal object, of a good-enough selfobject (though this latter term is not one that Spotnitz has utilized). This is a concept that, in some ways, is conceptually difficult to apply to batterers, but one that clinical experience with many batterers and violent couples has convinced me is a potentially valuable one to pursue. It is an idea that may neatly bridge the Spotnitzian concept of narcissistic defense with the Kohutian ones of narcissistic equilibrium and rage. The narcissistic defense is eminently clear in batterers when we observe them justify all kinds of atrocious treatment suffered as children.

Some batterers will state that they often deserved to be beaten, due to some transgression on their parts. (There are less obvious versions of this defense in the batterer, but none presenting the aforementioned theoretical problem.) This protects them from being consciously flooded by the wealth of traumata or traumatic themes (Shabad 1993), or the affect attendant to it, that they would encounter in the event of a breakdown of the narcissistic defense. It is my impression that battering is employed when the integrity of the narcissistic defense is acutely failing. It is this use of the narcissistic defense that is conceptually difficult. I attempted an exposition of this idea earlier (Scalia 1998). But I struggle further with it now, as it may be inseparably related to the immediacy and potentially life-threatening nature of narcissistic rage.

As batterers are enduring what they experience as an attack by their spouse, they find the spouse's attack to resonate to early pathogenic experiences they defended against narcissistically, i.e., by attacking themselves so as to protect a good-enough image or representation of the object: "If it is my fault, and it must be, then I have a chance of improving the treatment I receive, by changing myself." (Or, alternatively, "Then I can at least imagine [hallucinate] a good-enough object.") "I can believe that the object is good. And of course, this way I can feel sustained by maintaining inside myself this good object representation." Inasmuch as the spouse serves projectively for them as that good object, and to the extent that they attempt to maintain a perception of the spouse as consonant with that early object representation (i.e., by attempting to force the spouse to comply with it), that spouse is now failing to cooperate with the batterer's vision. Based on the batterer's current perception of his spouse as deriding him, she is felt to undermine the cohesiveness of his original narcissistic defense. They are phenomenologically being treated in the original pathogenic ways. All pathogenic traumata, as well as any real or imagined trauma currently being inflicted upon them, threaten to converge instantaneously, which would entirely overwhelm the stimulus barrier and theoretically create a neuropsychological experience of termination of the very existence of the self. (In fact, in this latter regard, a few batterers appear unable to recall parts or all of battering incidents, possibly because of an actualized, temporary neuropsychological termination of the existence of self.)

If this is view is correct, it would be subjectively experienced as highly dangerous, a crisis that must be averted. (The similarity to the threat of the loss of narcissistic equilibrium, to the threat of the loss of the selfobject, I trust, is obvious.) Thus all rage ever directed against the self, all self-attack that has ever protected the good-object representation, the good inner object, is mobilized against the currently perceived new threat. It is as though the batterer is saying to himself, were he able: *This event is too much like how I was repeatedly mistreated growing up. The only way to have tolerated it then, the only way to have had any hope at all of surviving and acquiring needed love, admiration, and security was to believe that I somehow was causing this maltreatment by those whom I needed to love, admire, and protect me. I had to believe that I was worthless, as worthless as the rotten way in which I was being treated suggested. At least then there remained the hope that I could change things. If I could improve myself, I could be treated better; and I could thus believe that my parents were good enough. I blamed myself in order to salvage my image of them. Now those old intolerable abnegations are "in my face" again! (My spouse) is making me feel then-and-now all at once! I am being "smeared out" (one of my patients' terms for it) of existence!! I am not so bad as I have told myself! And there is a loving object in there (in me)!! (My spouse) just wants to destroy it! No! I won't allow it! I will survive, and this damnable one must be destroyed, to do no more harm!!* The battered spouse has become the split-off, persecuting, rejecting object. Could this be the vehicle of Kohut's *narcissistic* rage?

CHAPTER TWO

THE EXPERIENCE OF SELF AND OTHER

The advances in psychoanalysis over recent decades are so great that it is staggering and daunting for any one individual to attempt to assimilate them. Representative of some of these changes is the impact of the works of Margaret Mahler and Daniel Stern, elaborated by many authors.[1] Both theoreticians' conflation of observational research and psychoanalytic theory have yielded rich material. While in some ways their contributions are divergent, I will attempt to synthesize them here insofar as they are germane to the understanding and treatment of domestically violent individuals.

THE WORK OF DANIEL STERN AND BATTERERS

For over a decade ago now, Daniel Stern has compiled an impressive, multifaceted compendium (1985). He catalogued the leading infant research up to the time of his writing, providing a highly useful manual as well as a review of the history of psychoanalysis's infant theories and their attendant effects on clinical practice. He addressed the notion of inference of an "observed infant" (i.e., the actual infant that one may directly observe) from our experiences with the "clinical infant" (i.e., clinically manifest psychopathology as assumed infantile sequelae in our adult patients). Finally, he posited a new psychoanalytic developmental psychology made possible by these perspectives, combined with the work of self psychologists (as exemplified by Kohut 1972 and Wolf 1988). Not accidently, Stern's work lends itself to a particularly experience-near psychoanalytic theory of pathogenesis.

Rather than stages, or phases, of development, Stern prefers to speak of *domains* of relatedness.

All domains of relatedness remain active during development. The infant does not grow out of any of them; none of them atrophy, none become developmentally obsolete or get left behind. And once all domains are available, there is no assurance that any one domain will necessarily claim preponderance during any particular age period. None has a privileged status all of the time. Since there is an orderly temporal succession of emergence of each domain during development—first *emergent*, then *core*, then *subjective*, then *verbal*—there will inevitably be periods when one or two domains hold predominance by default. In fact, each successive organizing subjective perspective requires the preceding one as a precursor. Once formed, the domains remain forever as distinct forms of experiencing social life and self. None are lost to adult experience. Each simply gets more elaborated. (31–32)

Inasmuch as I consider the senses of both core self and subjective self to be those domains of relatedness that are disrupted in relation to battering, as well as its nonphysical, interpersonal precursors, it will be these domains to which I give the most attention. First, however, it will be helpful to clarify the meanings of the senses of an emergent self and a verbal self, as Stern posits them.

Until the shift into the sense of a core self occurs, "the infant is generally thought to occupy some kind of presocial, precognitive, preorganized life phase that stretches from birth to two months" (Stern 1985:37). This is the period of an emergent self, roughly analogous to Mahler's autistic phase. For Stern the notion of a sense of self during this period must be considered, even though infants cannot thus consider themselves, since "they have separate, unrelated experiences that have yet to be integrated into one embracing perspective" (45). Whereas Stern is suggesting that we must attend to the infant's experiences themselves, previous research and theory have focused on the product of the infant's experience.

Can the infant experience not only the sense of an organization already formed and grasped, but the coming-into-being of an organization? I am suggesting that the infant can experience the *process* of emerging organization as well as the result, and it is this experience of emerging organization that I call the *emergent sense of self*. It is the experience of a process as well as a product. (45)

In order to fully appreciate the verbal sense of self, one must also grasp the concepts of the two preceding senses of self; we must grasp how the core self and subjective self evolve. But for now:

During the second year of the infant's life language emerges, and in the process the senses of self and other acquire new attributes. Now the self and the other have different and distinct personal world knowledge as well as a new medium of exchange with which to create shared meanings. A new organizing subjective perspective emerges and opens a new domain of relatedness. The possible ways of "being with" another increase enormously. At first glance, language appears to be a straightforward advantage for the augmentation of personal experience. But in fact language is a double-edged sword. It also makes some parts of our experience less shareable with ourselves and with others. It drives a wedge between two simultaneous forms of interpersonal experience: as it is lived and as it is verbally represented. Experience in the domains of emergent, core, and intersubjective relatedness, which continue irrespective of language, can be embraced only very partially in the domain of verbal relatedness. *And to the extent that events in the domain of verbal relatedness are held to be what has really happened, experiences in these other domains suffer an alienation.* (162–163; emphasis added)

In domestic violence, it is the batterer's, and most often both spouses', verbal rendition of their inner experience that is lost to them. That is, they are desperately and self-protectively attempting to verbalize and conceptualize an inner experience of an interpersonal event (borne of now *and* then) of intolerable proportions and attributes, but they are far removed (alienated in Stern's sense) from the actuality of their own experience. One of the unfortunate consequences of this fact is the blaming of the spouse for one's own intolerable inner experiences, which cannot be acknowledged and identified as such.

THE CORE SENSE OF SELF

Stern tells us:

The age of two months is almost as clear a boundary as birth itself. At about eight weeks, infants undergo a qualitative change: they begin to make direct eye-to-eye contact. Shortly thereafter they begin to smile more frequently, but also responsively and infectiously. They begin to coo. In fact, much more goes on during this developmental shift than what is reflected by increased overt social behaviors. Strategies for paying attention to the world shift in terms of altered visual scanning patterns. Motor patterns mature. Sensorimotor intelligence reaches a higher level, as Piaget has described. Electroencephalograms reveal major changes. Diurnal hormonal milieu stabilizes, along with sleep and activity cycles. Almost everything changes. (37)

Here we see that the infant has his first organizing subjective perspective about the self, though at a fairly basic level. Stern cites four *self-invariants* as the necessary components for the development of an organized sense of a core self. These are self-agency, self-coherence, self-affectivity, and self-history.

Self-agency is 1. the sense of being the source of one's own actions and 2. the sense of *not* being at the source of others' actions. Of course, this is a major developmental advance with tremendous social and interpersonal implications. Self-coherence is the sense of being a coherent, physical, delimited whole entity, while mobile or immobile. This also has prodigious implications and is at the core of much intimate violence. Self-affectivity is the experience of affects belonging to experiences of self. For the batterer, then, we may wonder, "When he or she feels a sense of angst, or painfully unrequitable longing, can it be recognized as an experience that ultimately originates from within, or does its origin seem to merge with the universe, in a kind of psychotic derealization?" And self-history is "the sense of enduring, of a continuity with one's own past so that one 'goes on being' and can even change while remaining the same. The infant notes regularities in the flow of events" (71). The sense of a core self is experiential, palpable vis-à-vis sensation, affect, substance, action, and time. Thus, it is foremost a "physical self that is experienced as a coherent, willful, physical entity with a unique affective life and history that belong to it. This generally operates outside of awareness. It is taken for granted, and even verbalizing about it is difficult" (26). I suggest that, leading up to and during battering, it is predominantly this sense of a core self that is disrupted. Yet it is necessary that one have an understanding of the other side of the coin, i.e. , that of the core self in relation to other, or of the self in relation to the self-regulating other.

One who regulates the infant's self experience is termed by Stern a *self-regulating other*.[2] Arousal, affect intensity, security, and attachment are among the vital self experiences that are co-created by the infant and the primary caregiver.[3] They are among the experiences largely managed by the self-regulating other. We might also think of a *somatic state regulating other*, inasmuch as a great deal of the sense of core self is experienced physically. The manner in which the self-regulating other, or the mother, attends to the infant will build up strong feelings and vitally important representations in the infant. Christopher Bollas (1987) refers to this function of the mother as that of a *transformational object*, which occurs largely pre-representationally, i.e., it does not yield symbolic representations but rather mnemic traces that constitute one's *aesthetic* of self-care and of foundational relating to the other, and to the object world in general. It is my contention that the batterer's experience of a self in relation to a self-regulating other has had serious disruptions over and over again, building up representations and/or mnemic traces embedded in one's character and in one's aesthetic, in one's *unthought* [but] *known* (Bollas 1987) expectational set for taking in and processing experience. Batterers expect others to be suddenly dangerous, toxic, overstimulating, attacking, fragmenting, filled or punctuated with moments of intense anxiety of a primitive, agonizing, overwhelming nature. Stern elaborates:

> The sense of a core self, since it is a dynamic equilibrium, is always in potential jeopardy. And indeed, it is a common life event to experience and/or feel major perturbations in the sense of a core self. Winnicott has made a list of what he calls "primitive agonies" or "unthinkable anxieties" to which children are heir. These are "going to pieces," "having no relation to the body," "having no orientation," "falling forever," "not going on being," and "complete isolation because of there being no means of communication." (199–200; Winnicott 1958, 1965, 1971)

It is when these states threaten to impinge upon the core self that battering or its precursors occur.

We can think of Puck as enduring such a crisis when the padlock had to be taken off his door. Or Jacques when he had to come indoors from a flirtation with an attractive girl in the neighborhood. Or Matt when he was impelled to jump up and menacingly rear back his fist.

Regarding the manner in which such inner states are activated, Stern tells us:

> Lived episodes (especially from childhood) immediately become the specific episodes for memory, and with repetition they become . . . generalized episodes of interactive experience that are mentally represented—that is, representations of interactions that have been generalized, or RIGs. . . . The experience of being with a self-regulating other forms RIGs. And these memories are retrievable whenever one of the attributes of the RIG is present. . . . Attributes are . . . recall cues to reactivate the lived experience. And whenever

a[n] RIG is activated, it packs some of the wallop of the originally lived experience in the form of an active memory. . . . The activation of different RIGs can influence different regulatory functions, ranging from the biological and physiological to the psychic. (110–111)

So, for example, let us say that a particular batterer's wife merely responds to a request of his with something of a mixed message. He asks her if she'd like to go out to dinner with him, and the way she, while verbally indicating her desire for dinner, indicates through her tone of voice some reluctance. Perhaps she suspects that dinner will deteriorate into an unpleasant evening, or is worried about spending the money, or even unconsciously wishes to make him feel unwanted or emasculated. Whatever the reason, it is her telling and its dissonance with its wording that disturb him. Assume that when he was growing up, a common and childhood-representative experience was of the following sort. He was an exuberant little boy who delighted in seeking out his mother's admiration for his youthful accomplishments, but heall too often encountered, "Yes, honey, that's nice," her telling indicating more of an "OK, dear, but Mother really isn't interested; what I am engaged in is much more important to me." Therein, the contrasting verbal and intersubjective or affective messages, and the feeling of rejection attendant on the emotional message, would constitute the basis of an RIG, or representation of interactions that will become generalized over time. So when this grown man's wife responds less than enthusiastically, the RIG is activated. As though "it" is happening currently, all of the emotions linked to that RIG are activated.

THE DISRUPTION OF THE CORE SELF

How is it that we are able only to see an interpersonal disruption in intersubjective relatedness, yet presume, know, or infer that there is also a disruption in the domain of core relatedness? The sense of a core self, which begins its establishment considerably earlier than any capacity for cognitive appraisal exists, bases its judgments on affective appraisals of situations. This core self, which is superseded by a sense of a subjective self, nevertheless continues its existence within each of us throughout our lives. Such disruptions can be experienced as nonlocalizable distress, incapable of being sorted out cognitively. Bollas (1987) refers to "moods" as such a phenomenon, moods being manifestations of our having conserved within ourselves mnemic traces of the earliest object. Yet our verbal selves always attempt to attribute verbally construed meaning to experience. If the batterer attempts to locate the source of his distress within current interactions or experiences, he is necessarily going to obfuscate a significant part of the picture and, as discussed, be prone to blame his spouse or child for his own disruption.

Let us say that our subject grew up in a home that was affectively characterized by the following. Mother was depressed a good deal of the time when he was an infant. She also suffered severe anxieties herself; being separated from her own family of origin, which she idealized, but which in truth left her quite energically depleted, and having had to form a "false self" relationship to her world so as to fend off her own "primitive agonies," she entered young adulthood ill-equipped to feel secure or fulfilled—yet these experiences were kept out of awareness. Consider that she and her young husband fought intensely. He came from a family that was highly neglectful and also abusive—sexually, verbally, physically. He too entered adulthood with serious deficits in his capacity to embrace life openly, fully, and with his own considerable "false self" adjustment. These two young spouses clung to each other during those times at which they were not actively alienated from one another.

Our future batterer's home atmosphere during the emergence of his sense of a core self was characterized by what would later lead to his battering. Perhaps the father would handle the children too roughly when their crying precipitated disintegration anxieties in him. They might have often been left alone in their cribs while the mother and father were in the throes of one of their hours-long fights. Perhaps only marginal, periodic attention was then available, at best. One would certainly then be filled with the intense aggression and persecutory and disintegration anxieties that were then suffusing the home, inundating the atmosphere. And this when the children ought to have been comforted, rocked, fed, cooed at, smiled at, "met" well, attunedly to their needs and inner states. At other times, the mother might have used the infant in a self-comforting holding, in a manner that still failed to attend to the actuality of the infant's, the future batterer's, psychic needs.

As they moved through the domains of intersubjective and verbal relatedness, did they learn to submerge "true self" in efforts to gain what they could from parents who were dramatically failing to attend properly to them? What kinds of affective experiences populated the emergences and ongoing existences of all their domains of relatedness? What I am intending to hypothesize is that in the domain of core relatedness their subjective

experiences were highly characterized by physiological states that attend imminent severe physical danger (during rough handling or when they were too close to the emotional or physical violence that often transpired between their parents). Also imbuing their establishment of core related-ness were distressing states of interpersonal isolation when neither parent had the cognizance or emotional wherewithal to be attendant to them. As their capacities for intersubjective and verbal relatedness were emerging, they had already learned that there was no solace to be gained from either parent for their most distressing inner states. Neither parent could allow or provide for any representation or transformation of these states. The fate of the capacity for symbolic representation, and its failed development as manifest in the establishment of the *terminal object* and its implications (Bollas 1995), when trauma or cumulative trauma dominates a given cluster of experiences, will be dealt with in parts 2 and 3. For now, let us realize that affects experienced in the climate I describe constitute primitive agonies and unthinkable anxieties. Winnicott called them psychotic anxieties, highlighting the imminent threat of disintegration the batterer is struggling against. Perhaps even more saliently descriptive a phrase for the affective threat to the batterer is not merely the fear of "going to pieces," but that of "flying to pieces," or "being exploded to pieces." *Thus, to prevent the inner experience of "being exploded to pieces," batterers explode externally at the other, externalizing the threat and the experience, where they have some chance of managing it, controlling it. Indeed, parenthetically one might wonder whether such a flight from disintegrative-persecutory anxiety always conjoins "identification with the aggressor."*
Stern distinguishes:

> In clinical terms, some patients have a relatively well-formed sense of a core self, which is stable but requires an enormous amount of maintaining input, in the form of both phasic and tonic contributions from others. When that input fails, the sense of self falls apart. Others have a less well-formed sense of self which, while equally stable, requires much less maintenance. And still others are most characterized by a great lability of this sense of self that cannot be fully explained by changes in maintaining input. (200)

Matt demonstrated this latter phenomenon in my office, much to my surprise and fright, in the context of the recently begun couples therapy discussed earlier. I have no idea what precipitated his outer or his inner response, but, suddenly, from what appeared to be a wholly unimpinging situation for him, he erupted into an intense rage and was standing over me, his fist cocked back, ready to strike me in the face. He is the only batterer who has ever been so overtly and imminently threatening to me. Paradoxically enough, this event served as a springboard for both of us, giving us a shared event through which to identify his disintegration anxiety and from which we began an individual psychotherapy of some four years' duration now.

Matt had been terribly neglected and physically abused as a child, and his upbringing made egregious circumstances seem normal. Thus, he had no voice, no capacity for cognitive appraisal or recognition of the evocation of a most disturbing and dangerous RIG. He could only point to what precipitated his unthinkable anxieties in a given situation, and he considered these to be causes rather than triggers of his current distress. He would then attempt to eradicate the affectively appraised annihilating danger. At this point in his therapy, which is limited by a weekly or often once every two or more weeks frequency (financial considerations imposing so), he appears caught in a largely *terminal object*—pre-occupied space, largely unable to free associate, largely unable to be actively curious about his self-foreclosing lifestyle. However, he does appear quite behaviorally contained with regard to violence, for the time being, having been violence-free for about two years now.[4] He also appears well ensconced in a narcissistic (idealizing) transference, allowing him to incrementally establish ego strengths previously unavailable to him. These nascent strengths are beginning to allow inchoate observations of and curiosities about himself that had been unthinkable earlier. Most especially, he can consider the destructiveness of his violence—along with its self-agency and self-affectivity—and ways that he uses events in his life as routes to passionate lament rather than self-transformation.

However, I have no doubt that he is still at risk of a violent eruption. In terms of an imagined overall course of analytic treatment, he has just begun. He largely eschews the paternal order, has very little reliable inner father, and uses me for more maternal function than anything else: a long road.

Jacques, whose stepfather was sentenced to the state prison for almost killing him, had a well-documented history given me by Child Protective Services when he arrived for treatment at fourteen, just recovered from his life-threatening wound. His mother was incestuously provocative, openly condoned or excused most of the stepfather's abuse, was herself intensely intermittently explosive toward her son as well as physically violent toward him, and reported a history of extant severe drug abuse from before Jacques's birth (though she insists she was drug-free during his gestation; fetal alcohol signs, at any rate, were not discernible). Jacques was himself already physically and sexually abusive toward vulnerable children and highly sexualized, and he sexually maltreated his numerous partners, demonstrating no remorse whatsoever.[5] After the life-threatening assault, Jacques's mother stood by her husband's side in a manner that left her son wholly abandoned yet unable to acknowledge or recognize she was doing anything harmful. Indications are that he experienced relatively severe abuse and neglect as an infant, though reports are conflicting and unreliable. Clearly, environmental determinants of a core self were violently disrupted in his life, as well exemplified in the near murder by his stepfather. We can imagine Jacques's struggling for his life after the assault; we can imagine his experiences of abject fear any number of times as his stepfather, a physically powerful man, beat him with his fists from an early age. We can imagine his humiliation when his stepfather slung countless racial epithets at him. What core self underpinnings!

Being of mixed racial heritage—Native American and white—Jacques was later to organize an indignant identity around racial inequities and injustices. These became knee-jerk, unimaginative rallying cries, justified or ill-placed, as only chance would have it. He would seek out instances of perceived racism and become a kind of champion of the underdog. He needed to find such events in order to define a sense of core self. As trauma became for him, very early on, life defining, so did he seek new instances of traumas. They gave him a sense of aliveness that was not well-developed psychostructurally. One day he came in to see me, livid in response to positive remarks made about Christopher Columbus on Columbus Day; he was sure that either the teacher had meant the remarks as a slight to Native Americans or that the teacher's lack of sensibility about such a matter constituted an egregious insult, deserving to be met with great force, though he could only fathom violent responses. Such violence and his thoughts of it appear to place him back into family life and contact with the part of him that was lost at the juncture of violence's entry into his life. It is as though communion with violence restores contact with a sense of true self that was lost pursuant to this same violence. In *The Shadow of the Object* Bollas (1987)—discussing the importance of reaching a patient "inside" a mood and applicable in this instance, as I see it—puts it this way: "It is my view that this often means contacting part of the individual's true self, but a true self that may be frozen at a time when self experience was traumatically arrested, and which sustains the child's rapport with his parents and his loss of personal reality" (112). And: "A conservative object frequently serves an important function in analysis when it preserves a self state that prevailed in the child's life just at the moment when the child felt he lost contact with the parents" (113). Bollas is talking here about moods as "conservative objects," and I believe that Jacques's sense of indignation can thus be understood. Bollas defines and explains: "Moods typical of a person's character frequently conserve something that was but is no longer. I will call that experience-memory stored in the internal world a conservative object. A conservative object is a being state preserved intact within a person's internal world: it is not intended to change, and acts as a mnemic container of a particular self state conserved because it is linked to the child self's continuing negotiation with some aspect of the early parental environment" (110).

Having been the butt of numerous racial epithets throughout his life, insults levied by his stepfather, and having experienced repeated incidents of physical violence by this man, along with a vast array of psychological torments that I will describe in more detail, it is not difficult to see how traumas could have come to be experienced not as events in his life but as life defining, as Bollas puts it.

The violence and violation that such experiences do to a human being is "unthinkable," very deeply disturbing, violently and nauseatingly disturbing. It moves primitive phantastical anxieties squarely into the realm of the Real, where they cannot be processed. Large segments of the self inevitably organize in manifold ways around the trauma, constituting a terminal inner object-relational world that forecloses the possibility of the self's elaboration or structural evolution in these realms, as the inner space in which such movement might occur is already occupied by the trauma.[6] Thus it is pre-occupied, or appropriated, before the self can find space for its generation. Jacques exploited racial justice as a kind of substitute, though inadequate, transformational object.

No real solace was ever really given him for the highly overstimulating (chapter 1) incursions into his sense of a core self, his experiences of annihilated self-cohesion. How does one form any kind of reliable, pliable, healthy intersubjective or verbal relatedness against or over a template of this kind of core self experience?

THE CONTRIBUTIONS OF MARGARET MAHLER AS PERTAINING TO BATTERERS

Much of what Mahler describes about both observed and clinical infants can be reliably understood from the conceptual standpoint of the clinical infant alone.[7] Her descriptions have a rich representational power of defensive internal object relations. It is from this latter perspective that we will draw on Mahler's work (Mahler, Pine, and Bergman 1975) to lend a clearer picture of the defensive operations and internal object relations of the batterer, or at least of the individual in a battering mode of operation (i.e., battering and its precursors).

AUTISM, SYMBIOSIS, AND SEPARATION-INDIVIDUATION

The normal autistic phase, thought to occupy the first month of life, sees the infant as a primarily biological organism that attempts to maintain its homeostatic equilibrium. Mahler considered there to be no discrimination between the subjective inside and the subjective outside, and none between animate and inanimate. Need satisfaction was presumed to be ascribed to itself by the infant, who was thought to reside in an omnipotent autistic orbit.

> Symbiosis refers to a stage of sociobiological interdependence between the 1- to 5-month-old infant and his mother, a stage of preobject or need-satisfying relationship, in which self and maternal intrapsychic representations have not yet been differentiated. From the second month on, the infant behaves and functions as though he and his mother were an omnipotent dual unity within one common boundary. (Mahler, Pine, and Bergman 1975:290–291)

"Any unpleasurable perception, external or internal, is projected beyond the common boundary of the symbiotic *milieu interieur* . . . [and thus] protects the rudimentary ego from stress traumata" (44–45). This last point is particularly germane to the mechanisms of domestic violence.

Separation-individuation is considered the lengthy two-year process of the individual's emergence from an initial symbiotic orbit into a solidly differentiated entity, capable of many ego functions, but, especially in regard to our considerations, the separated and individuated being is capable of a tolerance for ambivalence, experiencing frustrating and gratifying input from an other and recognizing the existence of the whole other within those experiences. Such an individual is then capable of recognizing the boundaries between oneself and an other, and is thus also capable of empathy. Also inherent in this advance is the capacity of waiting for gratification from or connection with the other when these are not immediately forthcoming. The child recognizes that the needed other will return, when he or she is absent, or recognizes that good experiences with the other will resume, while tolerating unpleasant experiences with the other. They are capable of emotional object constancy.

OBJECT CONSTANCY

The establishment of affective (emotional) object constancy (Hartmann 1952) depends upon the gradual internalization of a constant, positively cathected, inner image of the mother. . . . Emotional object constancy will, of course, be based in the first place in the cognitive achievement of the permanent object, but all other aspects of the child's personality development participate in this evolution as well. . . . The last subphase [of the separation-individuation phase] (roughly the third year of life) is an extremely important intrapsychic developmental period, in the course of which a stable sense of entity (self boundaries) is attained. . . . But the constancy of the object implies more than the maintenance of the representation of the absent love object. . . . It also implies the unifying of the "good" and the "bad" object into one whole representation. This fosters the fusion of the aggressive and libidinal drives and tempers the hatred for the object when aggression is intense. (Mahler, Pine, and Bergman 1975:109–110)

The implications for our consideration of the battering patient are here quite profound and will also be further discussed. However, attendant to object constancy, and to our concerns regarding an individual being able to act violently toward a usually loved someone, is the concept of "splitting," which requires some attention at this point. Though the term is by now widely used and has already been addressed to some degree, it needs clarification through the ideas of Melanie Klein, who gave us its early theoretical and clinical elaboration and deployment. Mahler (1975) defines it as "a defense mechanism often found during the rapproachment subphase [of separation-individuation, deployed when] the toddler cannot easily tolerate simultaneous love and hate feelings toward the same person. . . . Mother is experienced alternately as all good or all bad. Hence, the toddler may displace aggression onto the nonmother world while exaggerating love for (overidealizing) the absent, longed-for mother" (292). Here again, the interpersonal ramifications for domestically violent couples are considerable.

PROJECTION, PROJECTIVE IDENTIFICATION, AND COMPLEMENTARY PROJECTIVE IDENTIFICATION IN DOMESTICALLY VIOLENT COUPLES

In projection, one perceives a disavowed and split-off aspect of experience to exist outside of the self or the other. So, for example, one might project all-bad (overly negatively assessed and allowing of no consideration for concomitant goodness) or all-good (overidealized and allowing of no consideration of imperfection or frustration-source) split aspects of mother, or of one's spouse, onto some other person or entity. The child might attribute intolerably frustrating or rejecting experiences to an other upon whom he or she is not dependent. A husband or wife might project the sexually desirable experience of their spouse onto another, being unable to feel sustained sexual interest in the person upon whom they are most dependent for pregenital intimacy needs. A husband might project onto his wife currently evoked, i.e., precipitated, intolerable, though disavowed early childhood experiences; these would be experiences that are activated by a present experience with his wife, but they are unneutralized and toxicones he also repudiates as belonging to a different era; he experiences these as though they were happening now. This is very similar to Stern's RIGs, although the RIG concept does not lend itself so well to that of projective identification, which will be addressed momentarily. Similarly, and probably near universally in battering situations, a wife may simultaneously experience some interaction with her husband as though it were a collection of intolerable and defended against earlier experiences, but will attribute all attendent affect to the current behavior (or perception) of her husband. Projective identifications and complementary projective identifications can quickly make the situation quite complex.

Melanie Klein (1946), who gave us projective identification and explicated her theory, did not discuss the interpersonal and unconscious communication often concomitant with projective identification's deployment. Ogden (1982, 1986) has described it in an interpersonal manner, a description that lends itself well to couples dynamics, and particularly to domestically ones. His description is multifaceted. First of all, one must project a disavowed and split-off part-representation of oneself or of another. (Inasmuch as it is impossible to ever truly represent more than part of ourself, as Bollas [1992] so eloquently points out, it is understood that my usage here of part-representation is that situation in which the self suffers an inability to integrate competing and conflicting parts of itself.) Second, the projector acts in a manner, though this mechanism is outside of awareness, that places and expels intense experience squarely into the recipient of the projection, such that the recipient feels highly compelled to actually behave in a manner quite consonant with the projection.[8] At this point, the recipient has the potential options of either containing the powerful impulse to act out that which has been projected into him, or "put into" him,[9] or defending against the intense experience that pushes for discharge—i.e., one can then act out, or act out in a manner that grants the wished for discharge. However, if one does so, then the projector clearly has ample confirmation of the "accuracy" of his or her projection, as it has thus become "actualized" through enactment; the projector will not see the relative actuation of the event. Complementary projective identification, then, is theoretically merely the situation in which the projector-recipient scenario comes to occur bidirectionally. Hence, while A is putting pressure on B to act in concert with his projection, B is putting pressure on A to act in concert with her projection. The emotional intensity and identity confusion of such a situation is potentially enormous, annihilating, murderous.

For demonstration's sake, I will discuss a situation I observed on numerous occasions, in one form or another, in a young couple I was treating for domestic violence. The woman would often accuse the man of being passively malicious, passive-aggressiveness being one of his staple modes of interaction. However, she would at times wield this accusation when he was in fact attempting to warmly and vulnerably reach out to her. Her accusations of his malice were levied viciously, though this was outside of her awareness. She had no idea that she was herself behaving maliciously. It would usually not take him very long to begin to act in keeping with her accusations. She had a very strong histrionic propensity, which he would at times levy at her. Either one of them could and did initiate their rounds of complementary projective identifications and mutual blamings. While she was initially relatively calm and composed during her initiating flurry at him regarding his alleged passive malice, once he began to act in accord with this allegation—for example, taunting her with allegations of her overdramatizing and implying that she was out of touch with reality—she would rather quickly begin to enact his allegations. This is of course quite paradoxical, inasmuch as one outcome of this situation was that both of them were having to suffer the most unpleasant aspects of each other, which were in fact mutually and respectively provoked. Now had either one of them been able to contain the projective identifications coming from the other, the interpersonal outcome could have been quite different, even palliative. The treatment implications of these phenomena are considerable and potent.

While the capacity to contain these projective identifications might be rightly considered an ego-psychological arena of study and intervention, the matter is not so simple or easily dispatched. On first glance, it is alluringly attractive, for its sheer and relative ease of conceptual consideration, to assume that the individual failing to so contain is therein failing because of an ego deficit, as it were, or a relative lack of ego strength. Certainly, this is a legitimate line of consideration. However, it may well not circumscribe the story. Bollas's considerations of the conservative object and of the terminal object (1987, 1995) address ways by which the self unconsciously holds fast to overtly distressing and self-foreclosing states of being that are gratifying, though obviously not immediately observable. Thus, to give ever so brief an example, one might willingly (unconsciously) go into or remain in an overtly distressing interpersonal immediacy because it resurrects something of the poignant preoedipal past, longed for but lost. The distressing immediacy may provide an unconscious but powerful connection to the lost object of one's desire, while to find one's way clear to interpersonal harmony in the present would require a treaty with the self's present demands upon the past—a treaty that the self has not articulated and does not wish to articulate.

APPLICATIONS OF MAHLER

Let us now take a look at how object constancy disturbances, projective defenses against stress traumata, splitting, and disrupted empathy all converge to add to an eventuation of domestic violence. After doing so, we will return to Stern's contributions and examine the ways in which our Mahlerian considerations and those of Stern culminate in domestic violence, though still minus the requisite consideration of the batterer-universal defense of "identification with the aggressor."

In the battering couple we must imagine situations when ongoing (chronic) or situation-specific (acute) interactional experiences find one or both parties unable to maintain object constancy. One spouse is experienced in a way or ways that render the two unable to experience the emotional equivalent of knowing that they can "find the lost object," can resume a feeling of confident expectation, knowing that the current inner discomfort can be abated. When object constancy is unattainable, one cannot find a secure harbor within, cannot find an inner space from which to derive solace, cannot find a sanctuary in which hope is promised.[10]

By way of illustration, then, let us return to our passive-histrionic couple. Let us say that she cannot get herself "grounded" in any sense of trust that her inner disruption will be calmed, at least not once his passive-aggressiveness begins to drive home with much force. Her inner experience, then, is one of panic. The disruption is felt as highly dangerous, critical. Conversely, let us say that he cannot find any inner solace once her aggression becomes pitched, feverish, urgent. He feels and is centered on only the emotional emergency. At such points, whether one or the other has truly "started" the fight or not, both are acting toward each other based upon their respective character styles and character defenses. What has clearly happened and happens regularly for this couple is that their tenuous grips on object constancy are disrupted by the similarity (Stern's *evoked companion*) of a current encounter to a disavowed collection of traumatic events (Khan's [1963] *cumulative trauma*) during their formative years; this is decidedly *outside of awareness*. The negative, split-off, disavowed other of childhood (i.e., the cumulatively traumatizing parent[s]) has been emotionally conjured up with great intensity, and neither individual is now able to recover a sense of the internalizing soothing other.

This negative split-off representation of childhood and of the spouse (simultaneously) is now projected onto the spouse *as though* that is all the spouse is composed of. There can now be no empathy for the other, as, at this juncture, the actual other has ceased to exist in the self's immediate subjective experience. There is no modulation of hatred by noting or feeling that the currently hated or feared other is also the loved other, because object constancy is too disrupted at this juncture. It is intellectually amazing to observe couples at these times, to note how absolutely inaccessible they are, momentarily, to having the obvious pointed out to them. Nor does it matter how much, at calmer or more lucid moments, they can note a larger picture. *At this moment* they cannot do so. It is also amazing how difficult it is to "sit with" these couples at such times, especially when the therapist has been treating them long enough to be affected by the cumulative toxicity of all the interactions and has repeatedly experienced how impervious the couple is at these times to rational sense.

SELF PSYCHOLOGY AND OBJECT RELATIONS

Much can be said about the numerous theoretical and practical interfaces of Mahler's and Stern's work; most of that, of course, is far beyond the scope of this book.[11] However, there is a critical interface, one specifically germane here, that may now already be obvious, an interface at *the necessary theoretical confluence of a disrupted object constancy and of a disrupted sense of a core self*. What we must understand, in an experience-near way of theoretical conceptualization, is that many things occur internally in self experiencing when object constancy is severely disrupted. First of all, there are numerous concomitant and inextricably connected disturbances in ego function, such as sudden intensifications in the reliance on splitting and projective defenses, seriously impaired empathy, impaired ability to tolerate the inner experience of aloneness, disturbance in self-object differentiation, impaired observing-ego function, confusional states around past-present differentiation, etc. These are all important to note. However, what we ought to grasp well, for both theoretical and clinical reasons, is that one's narcissistic equilibrium and one's sense of a core self are being disrupted simultaneous with the disturbance in object constancy.

The subjective experience of this disruption is critical, primal, somatic, disturbing, terrifying, unable to be salved or soothed by cognitive means, whether these are interpretations, reassurances by an other, or contemplation by the self (who cannot then contemplate, as they are lost in *simple self experiencing* [Bollas 1992] at this moment). The disruption is preverbal, nonverbal, and is inaccessible to assistance via words or understanding. The self is gripped by the ineffable ghosts of the past, by what Bollas has called the *unthought known* (1987). In such a situation, whether or not it is immediately observable, the self is in a serious crisis in its attempt to maintain cohesion. There is a subjective threat that it will disintegrate, will "explode into pieces," in the phrase I like to modifiedly borrow from Winnicott. When a therapist has successfully managed to calm a patient in that situation numerous times, observing ego functions begin to develop around it, and verbal interventions begin to carry more sustenance, but only because they are experienced against a remembered background of the preverbal interventions that will by then have occurred many times.

Bollas (1987) speaks of the *transformational object* function of both the early mother and of the psychoanalyst. The infant child will have his experiences of being gradually transformed by the *good-enough* parent/mother, through thousands of somatic, psychic-somatic, interaffective, intersubjective interactions, *before* language acquires a transformational object capacity or registrability for the child. And likewise for the patient who is arrested around disturbances in the senses of self preceding Stern's sense of a verbal self—the fourth and highest form of self functioning. Insofar as battering pathology finds its origins within the emergent, core, and subjective senses of self, we must find intervention strategies and rationales that consider this *preverbal sense of self*.

If patients are to be treated within these pertinent pathognomonic venues, then we must be able to observe their existences. If therapists are to address the root motivating causes of domestic violence, and not throw these patients, battered and batterer alike, back into an untreated morass, they must address the preverbal disruptions in a far more sophisticated and demanding manner than the extant and still popular cognitive, psychoeducational, and consciousness-raising modalities undertaken, as they unwittingly implement wholesale neglect of the salient causal factors inherent in intimate violence.

CHAPTER THREE

IDENTIFICATION WITH THE AGGRESSOR

Once the batterer finds himself in the throes of intolerably disrupted object constancy and core self dissolution, there are still additional inner steps that must occur for him to resort to domestic violence, as there are many other internal and external possibilities potentially open to a given subject at this juncture. Anna Freud (1966 [1936]) tells us of the defense mechanism, popularized through her writing, of identification with the aggressor, that "[once a] criticism is internalized, the offense is externalized. This means that the mechanism of identification with the aggressor is supplemented by another defense mechanism, the projection of guilt" (118–119). This is clearly akin to what the contemporary victimology approach to domestic violence intervention refers to (more dyadic-descriptively) as blaming, which alone brings us no closer to understanding what is occurring within the batterer patient.

A few years ago, at a well-known and prestigious national conference on child abuse, I was struck by hearing a main speaker express chagrin at the lack of available knowledge regarding what ironically allows individuals who were themselves abused as children to later abuse ones less powerful than they. This speaker was befuddled by what appeared to him to be an inexplicable lack of empathy in such a scenario, for, in his thinking, shouldn't the current abuser instead be able to reflect upon how miserable it felt to to be so mistreated, and consequently elect, indeed wish, not to revisit such mistreatment upon any loved one? As troublingly pointed out in deMause's "The History of Child Abuse" (1998), the problem is that the now adult generation members must first be able to "live through their own childhood traumas a second time and work through their anxieties" (224) if there is not to be an "intergenerational transmission of a traumatic theme" (Shabad 1993).

However, to truly work through such traumas, as deMause and Shabad are suggesting, is a terribly painstaking, arduous, and lengthy process. What is more, the developing abused child usually has little or no opportunity to do so. Therefore, "instead of experiencing and integrating the negative feelings, the child incorporates those parts of the pain-producing person and acts as his perception of that person does" (Marshall 1982:130). The veracity of Marshall's statement was poignantly borne out by Jacques. Sadistically teased by his stepfather, he came to develop with unswerving likeness a pronounced pleasure at quite pointedly teasing children in order to torment them, children who had absolutely no more way of defending themselves than he had had with his stepfather. He would reduce little children to humiliated tears, suffering no guilt whatsoever, only glee at the other's pain. *Is a measure of a tormentor's glee a sense of joy at deliverance from their own sense of victimhood?* Anna Freud said,

> A child introjects some characteristic of an anxiety object and so assimilates an anxiety experience which he has just undergone. Here the mechanism of identification or introjection is combined with a second important mechanism. By impersonating the aggressor, assuming his attributes or imitating his aggression, the child transforms himself from the person threatened to the person who makes the threat. (113)

A few years earlier, Sandor Ferenczi, who for political reasons was to be denied acclaim for his pioneering work within and contributions to psychoanalysis, had written the following:

> The misused child changes into a mechanical, obedient automaton or becomes defiant. . . . For our theory this assumption is highly important—namely, that *the weak and undeveloped personality reacts to sudden unpleasure not by defense, but by anxiety-ridden identification and by introjection of the menacing person or aggressor.* Only with the help of this hypothesis can I understand why my patients refused so obstinately to follow my advice to react to unjust or unkind treatment with pain or with hatred or defence. One part of their personalities, possibly the nucleus, got stuck in its development at a level where it was unable to use the *alloplastic* way of reaction but could only react in an *autoplastic* way by a kind of mimicry. Thus, we arrive at the assumption of a kind of mind which . . . lacks the ability to maintain itself with stability in the face of unpleasure—in the same way that the immature find it unbearable to be left alone, without maternal care and without a considerable

amount of tenderness. Here we have to revert to some of the ideas developed by Freud a long time ago according to which the capacity for object-love must be preceded by a stage of identification. (1933:163)

I am struck by this passage of Ferenczi's, published long ago. It is so rich, both theoretically and clinically, it seems truly amazing that it has not been more widely disseminated, especially in light of a movement today to understand what drives all violence, including intimate violence. In the unpublished manuscript referred to earlier, Betcher and Ball (1997) found in the Chicago area that of nineteen batterers' therapists interviewed, three had not heard of identification with the aggressor, seven more were unable to define it, six were able to define it in their own terms, two were able to describe it by example, and one "chose to disregard this term due to a differing theoretical orientation." Of course, the implications for pursuant therapeutic intervention are worrisome.

Ferenczi spoke of the abused child's efforts to seek solace with the nonoffending parent, and the child being met with a refusal, with a denial of their efforts, in effect seeing their plea as nonsensical. If there is no solace provided and no validity given to the child's true experience of having been traumatized, identification with the aggressor becomes a reasonable and prudent coping strategy for the abused child, who will thus later behave abusively toward those dependent upon him and weaker than he is. Anna Freud expressed the mechanism this way:

An ego which with the aid of the defense mechanism of projection develops along this particular line introjects the authorities to whose criticism it is exposed and incorporates them in the superego. It is then able to project the prohibited impulses outward. Its intolerance of other people precedes its severity toward itself. It learns what is regarded as blameworthy but protects itself by means of this defense mechanism from unpleasant self-criticism. Vehement indignation at someone else's wrongdoing is the precursor of and substitute for guilty feelings on its own account. Its indignation increases automatically when the perception of its own guilt is imminent. (119)

Hanna Segal (1973 [1964]), discussing the work of Melanie Klein, speaks in this vein: the subject wards off depressive anxiety over worry that its impulses may be damaging the internal object, and oneself—as the object is needed for survival—by the employment of a manic defense. The depressive anxiety and guilt over the fear that one has irretrievably damaged the object upon whom the subject depends is defended against with the primitive mechanisms of splitting, projective identification, denial, idealization, etc. This situation obtains when the subject has achieved a sense of the wholeness of the other and is capable of *ambivalence*, conflict over the direction of contrasting good and bad impulses that can now be understood as directed at one and the same entity—originally the mother. This is part of the situation of the *depressive position*, whereas in the earlier *paranoid-schizoid position* the self's splitting function is more absolute; there is practically no knowing that the object of one's aggression is the same mother who is also the object of one's desire, and there is thus no concern that one's aggressive impulses could damage what one desires. Thus when the manic defense is employed, it is constituted by an aggregation of control, triumph, and contempt. The value of the loved object is denied, even seen as contemptible and pointedly not as something one is dependent upon. Hanna Segal asserts that control, which we know to be so prevalent among batterers in their relations with the objects of their dependency needs, allows the subject to simultaneously deny dependence upon the object and compel it to meet dependency needs. The sense of triumph follows the denial and dismissal of dependency, of valuing and caring for the object; the desired but dangerous object of longing and unrequited desire is thereby defeated. Segal believes that contempt obliterates the self's sense of its object's being worthy of guilt, with this contempt then also serving as a justification for further attacks upon the denied, longed for object.

Eight-year-old Albert exhibits regular manic feasts, as Freud called them. He is often unremorsefully violent with his adoptive mother and, reportedly, regularly experiences the manic triad just discussed. When he first came to his adoptive family as a foster child of three, he had been taken from an alcoholic single mother who often left him locked inside the house, so that he could not exit, while she went out in search of drink and parties. She was rather grossly neglectful of him; there were reports of his roaming his neighborhood unattended—when she *was* at home—and ending up blocks from home by age two, and she often used a wooden paddle, which he remembers, in the execution of corporal punishment. There is much more to the story, but this will meet our purposes. For the first two years of his foster care, he appeared quite attached to his foster mother, who doted on him, and it was conceivable that he was building up an internal sense of the object's goodness and reliability—one of the main developmental tasks of the paranoid-schizoid position. In the ensuing two to three years, the warmth and affection between them has progressively eroded, until now he has quite alienated his adoptive mother, seeming unconcerned about her, while she has a predominantly negative experience of him—a situation that was far from the case earlier on. He has also begun to display certain other behaviors that give cause for worry about his developing an antisocial adjustment. The parents are now considering sending him to analysis at the rate of three times a week, the minimum at which I feel I could have a reasonable analytic chance of altering his course by puberty. Otherwise, he is quite on his way to becoming a batterer, as were both his biological parents.

If I get the opportunity to treat him analytically, will the devolving analytic story reveal that he has a genuine concern for the object, a concern concealed by a manic defense, or will he prove himself to be more entrenched in a paranoid-schizoid posture? At any rate, I suggest that the answer is only attainable analytically, that is, through the revelation of his unconscious mind and his psychostructural constitution within the unraveling of his inner self and object world as occurs in a progressive psychoanalysis. By this point in time he has manically and magically reified aggression into a kind of identity

As I see it, identification with the aggressor is universal in batterers—all batterers are engaged in this defense, though not exclusively this defense, when they batter. It is employed as a protection from a current emotional experience that is reminiscent of—either through its actual or its misperceived similarity or a combination thereof—intolerable, originally battering-pathogenic experiences that the subject is affectively reminded of, even if outside awareness, by a current experience. Instead of allowing themselves to reexperience victimization subjectively, batterers "become" that which they originally felt victimized by. Ferenczi spoke of the subject's inability to maintain itself in the face of "unpleasure." But the batterer's unpleasure at this juncture is one of a keen disruption in the sense of a core self, in one's capacity for object constancy, in one's ability to rely upon the object's meeting of one's dependency needs. It is, to reiterate, a *keen* disruption, "keen" being defined by the American Heritage Dictionary as *having a fine, sharp cutting edge or point; intense, piercing.* They flee from knowledge of who the object of their desire and dependency really is; object constancy is obliterated and, with it, so too is the capacity for object-love.

What we appear to be facing in our batterer patients is a situation in which the "stage of identification which precedes object-love" was too marked by traumatic disruptions of security-anchoring experiences, of senses of self, of self in relation to (whole)other. Often, as Ferenczi has taught us, the only way of coping for these children was identification with the aggressor. This is also inextricably related to what the modern psychoanalytic school has termed the narcissistic defense (Spotnitz 1987 [1976]), in which the subject attacks itself for the object's transgressions against it, so as to preserve a good-enough inner representation of that important other. As I have said, many batterers tell us of rather egregious offenses perpetrated against them as children, by one or both parents, but then report that they are grateful to these parents for this harshness, citing (only too protestingly) how well these maltreatments helped rear them, helped them learn important lessons, that their parents were correct. They will often also tell us how effectively "spanking" and other corporal punishments "work" now to accomplish behavioral and attitudinal (quasi) compliance in their own children.

A BRIEF DIGRESSION: HARMFUL MYTHS

I should digress here long enough to at least theoretically dispel what I have found to be a near ubiquitous misperception among batterers' therapists (though this is beginning to be ameliorated with recent psychoanalytic forays into this patient domain) and battered women's advocates: the assumption that batterers batter capriciously and "because they can." I will take this opportunity to dispell the assumption that battering that leaves bruises on only parts of the body that can be concealed from public view serves as "proof" that batterers are "in control" of their violence, an assertion used to further the argument that one batters "because one can *and wants to.*"

Obviously, claiming that one batters merely because one can do so with impunity fails to address why anyone would be content to behave in such a manner; it assumes and implies that there is a conscious, knowing, and insouciant choice inherent in battering. Battering, as we have been discussing, is the outward manifestation of a visceral ego defense mechanism; as such, conscious control over oneself is compromised. Such compromise of self-control is not, however, the equivalent of complete loss of control. While battering, one might still be consciously present enough to attempt to salvage some measure of self-esteem, which is obviously compromised by one's battering behavior as well as the guilt and shame attendant on it. It is the shame and the effort to preserve some self-esteem that account for those times in which one batters in ways that leave hidden bruises. Parenthetically, I am not dismissing the fact that some individuals behave this way for motives other than those just suggested, but these are a different class of batterers and in fact are not batterers proper but sadistic psychopaths, which I believe comprise a very, very small percentage of persons who batter (and certainly of those who ever make it to a therapist's door, even when we are considering compulsory treatment). While having lost much self-control, a batterer may still have enough presence of mind and wherewithal to take some notice of where he leaves bruises or other signs of abuse.

IDENTIFICATION WITH THE AGGRESSOR AS DEFENSE AGAINST DISRUPTION IN CORE SELF AND IN OBJECT CONSTANCY

When the core self is acutely disrupted, when the patient feels a sufficient sense of object constancy slipping away, that is, when he comes to feel a dangerous degree of disintegration anxiety and the usual good-enough sense of solace and comfort unsummonable, then we will see a batterer protect himself internally by identification with the aggressor. Depending upon the severity and the pervasiveness of these disruptions in the patient's character, we will see this defense more or less often, more or less characterologically, and more or less intractably situated.

My patient, Matt, mentioned earlier, who drew his fist back against me in session, was, after two years of weekly sessions, still justifying a good deal of abusiveness. Matt's first few years of life were with parents who often waged tumultuous fights, the children being exposed to this. Corporal punishment was readily called upon in their home. After a divorce, when the patient was in his latency years, he found himself with a stepfather who grew progressively violent as Matt approached and then moved into adolescence; this violence grew into fisticuffs and more. The patient recalls one fight in which this stepfather threw him through a window, glass shattering everywhere. He reports another incident in which this man blindsided him coming around a corner—because he had a report from a neighbor that Matt had misbehaved in a minor way (which Matt says was even incorrect)—and he hit him in the head with a two-by-four, knocking him unconscious. His mother, too, was violent toward him when Matt was younger—for example, clubbing him on top of the head with a heavy brush with such force that she knocked him to the ground. He was also farmed out to the family ranch for months at a time and used as a ranch hand. To his credit, however, he did manage to fashion this into something of a transformational object, using nature as a constant object and finding solace there; to this day, he is an avid and competent outdoorsman.

When Matt is most threatened internally, he will, most intractably and intensely, invoke identification with the aggressor as a defense. For example, he is able to notice, after he gains some emotional distance from a situation, that he has spoken hurtfully and denigratingly to one of his sons, now feeling some degree of guilt and remorse. It is almost as if he evokes Mother Nature to assist him. Still, there remains an emotional distance from the full affective "hit" such a situation dredges up for him, and his empathy for that son, in that situation, remains limited. When his older, adult son initiated a physical altercation with him, he responded quickly in kind—the two men, father and son, punching and pushing one another. Although in some such situations he is able to experience some responsibility and remorse, in this situation he could feel none, not consciously, at any rate. He was unable to ascertain if he had done anything regrettable. This is a clear example of what Anna Freud meant when she pointed out that the projection of the self-attacking superego grows in severity and indignation the more the subject must defend himself against vehement self-criticism. So, theoretically, this patient can feel remorse more readily when his behavior is less damaging to the loved other, when there is less situation-inherent self-criticism for him to contend with. For him to note that he had failed his adult son by ending up in a violent physical altercation with him, for him to consciously perceive the tragedy of such a scene, to note the numerous and disturbing implications of this scene, would have been too much to bear at this juncture in his self development. Even the superego-modulating effects of the analyst were insufficient at this point to allow him to fully take in the scene; he would have been too brutal with himself for his conscious self to endure the onslaught. Of course, the analytic ego of the therapist will at times have to contend with his urge to be the voice of a punitive superego at such junctures. We may wish to speak up on behalf of the recipient of our patient's abusiveness; that is, we may tend to "identify with the victim" and argue on their behalf.[1] But we must beware, as so often it is not a case of a *lack* of superego but an overly *harsh* superego, with which our patient cannot contend, that we are really dealing with. If we try to be the voice of "justice," we will unwittingly create more harm than good. Aichhorn's and Eissler's messages quoted in the introduction remain quite unprocessed, undigested, unintegrated by us.

I think too of the account, of which I've written elsewhere (1994), of the father-son interaction I once witnessed in a retail shop in which the little boy was asking his father to buy him some object of his desire, and in which the boy did not readily enough, for the sake of his father's disturbed narcissistic equilibrium, stop the pleading as admonished by his father. The father decisively, preemptively, actually punched him in his head.[2] The father's violent and abrupt interdiction brought about an equally abrupt silencing of and capitulation by the son, who became still as stone, showing only shock as an outward sign of trauma. This little boy probably knew from numerous other experiences that should he fail to capitulate at this point that he would be in grave danger, or, more likely, he merely knew on an instinctual level, based on the ferocity of the father's blow and its attendant affect, that he was now in danger. He appeared to wholly accept his father's authority then. This father would probably tell us in treatment that his punch—a "knuckle punch"—worked, that is, it was successful in bringing about compliance, and that only such a method worked well with this difficult boy. Think of the potency of such events in cementing an identification with the aggressor defense. This boy had no way to be comforted, no way to be made safe from his father, no way to express the emotional flooding of the consequences of being so attacked, and of additionally enduring the reality of the attacker being his own father, no way to have his father not blame him for his being attacked. Being a robust little fellow, he will likely not have access to such character adaptations as depression, schizoid adjustment, passive-aggressiveness, or psychosomatic illness as potential primary coping strategies.[3] He will demonstrate identification with and introjection of his father's harsh attitudes and intolerance and will expect the same acquiescence from those less strong than himself that his father expected from him.[4] The powerful affects that were immediately averted when his father hit him will all come flooding back into self-experience whenever his wife or children do anything that challenges his ability to maintain his narcissistic equilibrium. He will defend against his inner states of disruption then by behaving the same way his father had with him. When successful, this exertion of abuse by violent patients, then, forces the other, e.g., one's spouse or one's child, back into compliance with ways of being that allow the subject to regain a cohesive sense of self- and of object-constancy. Here we find the "power and control" concern of the victimology approach, but it obviously falls short in helping us to understand our patients' experience. It protects us from the difficult task of studying what is really going on, protects us from the frequently ambiguous clinical picture, and allows us to exercise our own defense of identification with the aggressor, to shame patients in the name of expecting them to accept responsibility for their own behavior. But it does not negate the patients' emergency internal situations and their urgent need to require the other to assume the functions for them of being a good-enough mother substitute, of being a selfobject, of being a constant object.

No matter how much we may wish otherwise and no matter how much our own defenses may prevent us from noticing, the patient is unable at these junctures to be cognizant of and to "sit with" (contain) his disrupted equilibrium. Identification with the aggressor, whether we like it or not, is a defense mechanism that is as much outside awareness as all other defense mechanisms in action.

EXPULSION AND EXTERNALIZATION OF IMMINENT INTERNAL EXPLOSION

Just before battering occurs there is an internal explosion by which the subject is imminently threatened. This is the variation of Winnicott's "going to pieces" that I have already discussed. I am suggesting the distinction that the core self experience is a rising within of an intolerable pressure that feels as though it is about to blow one to pieces, as though there is an explosive device inside the self about to detonate.

One explosive mother would regularly experience this when her prepubescent son would attempt to assert an authority that challenged hers. She would attempt to extract compliance from him with a succession of progressively desperate measures until, sooner or later, she could not stand it and would violently strike out, with slapping or berating, intense affectivity, rage suffusing the very air, and rage suffusing her son.

Sally had been diagnosed as depressed, and was on anti-depressant medication. Her twelve-year-old son Peter had been taking Ritalin—for a (mis-)diagnosis of ADHD (attention deficit hyperactivity disorder)—a drug he had been taking since age four. This mother had an unconscious hatred of children that Peter registered on at least a core self level. She would often criticize him for what were merely his youthful exuberances, but then she would act as though nothing untoward had occurred. When he would object, she would quickly grow incensed and attempt to silence him, and when she was unsuccessful in that effort an escalation was fast in the making.

There was one incident in which he had come bounding down the stairs, excited to tell his father, Henri, of a TV history show about to begin, on a topic of interest they shared. Sally felt his excitement to be unsettling and caustically indicated how uncouth he was. "Aren't you ever going to learn to act like a gentleman? Stairs are for walking on, not for hopping on like some damned monkey!" Henri attempted to intervene on behalf of his son, but was his usually overwought self in the face of Sally's pronouncements of him as half-man at best, as someone who would never be as true a man as her own father. "And that son of yours is never going to be any better as long as you never get any balls!"

Trying to force her family to comply with her imagined maternal and paternal desires of her, Sally's fantasy was quickly dashed by Peter, whose bounding and calling out to his father was in direct opposition to the scene of a "dignified" and "mannered" ambience within which she attempted to picture herself. The harsh yanking it away from her, as she experienced Peter's spirited self in that moment of his merely anticipating a nice time with his dad, constituted a narcissistic and affective minicrisis for her, to which she reacted unthinkingly, attuned only to her inner object world. She was fighting off a self experience at the core self level of exploding into pieces.

Or Matt again. Matt began psychotherapy the day after the couples session in which he drew his fist back at me. His entry into an individual psychoanalytic psychotherapy occurred when I was able to let him feel that I understood his subjective experience in that situation and that I had no need to scold or humiliate him for it. It was this experience-near concept of "exploding into pieces" that allowed me to reach him. He felt more deeply understood than he ever had before. He was impressed by my understanding of what his experience had been and struck by its articulation, as he himself had never been able to do so. In his case, it was this knowledge that turned the tide and allowed a treatment-destructive moment to be transformed into the basis for a holding environment.

When Jacques exploded into the incredible rage discussed earlier, identification with the aggressor was obviously one defense mechanism mobilized at that moment. But what else happened within him for him to reach explosion status? This is the patient, it will be recalled, who endured years of intense abuse and was nearly killed by his stepfather. At some point in the staff-patient interaction, something "snapped" within him. We can easily conjecture that, in this situation, his stepfather's egregious violations of this young man's personal rights and freedoms bombarded him and reached "overload" status when he exploded. He was about to explode within, experience personal destruction, obliterate his own self, and "threw" the explosion outside of himself, expelled the "bomb," rationalizing his action with the belief that the source of the threat to himself was then external.

Since this *exploding into pieces* is such an experience-near concept, as I employed it with Matt, it can be used to help some patients articulate and thereby inaugurate becoming conversant with the inner locus of their difficulties. Rather than the patient's resorting to expulsion or obliteration in a necessarily mindless mental procedure, we hereby birth a new observing locale from which thought—mediating thought—serves as nascent *transformational object* to the batterer's fear of disintegration.

I am not proposing an unanchored cognitive-behavioral or interpretive wielding of this concept. In that vein, I'll allow Kohut to caution us, regarding our own misbehaviors, that when our efforts are rebuffed by our patients, "being narcissistically wounded, we tend to become enraged and then to rationalize our counterattacks in scientific, moral, or most frequently, morally tinged scientific terms" (1984:141). That is, our identifications with the victim or with society's laws must be well enough analyzed or contained if we are not to act out with these patients in a kind of secondary projective identification. To that end, I will now take up some of the ways that this very acting-out has become pervasive.

PART 2

THE POLITICS OF THE BATTERER-TREATMENT MOVEMENT

CHAPTER FOUR

POLITICAL VERSUS CLINICAL DETERMINATION OF ABUSE AND OTHER ASSOCIATIONS

The term *abuse* has become a hackneyed and often violent-innocently (Bollas 1992) appropriated one.[1] In an effort to deproblematize what needs to remain a crucial term in our shared lexicon, I will expound on some of what I have found to be destructive overassignations, underassignations, and dissemblingly unilateral assignations of this viscerally evocative word. Without considering these phenomena, we cannot heed Kohut's exhortation and would instead utilize the term as a tool for blaming, as a dissimulated deployment of persecutory aggression. There are several ways in which we use the term *abuse* to ignore disquieting complexities and to defend against a struggle with the containment of psychic states.[2]

In its overassignation misnomer, usually deployed in expression of a projective defense (*"I'm* not abusive, but *he* certainly is!") or in an identification with the victim, we see such rhetoric as the following. In the typical invoking of the label, overt behaviors of any sort might be identified. Pushing, restraining, shoving, barring one's entry or exit are often cited as forms of physical abuse or domestic violence. Or, if one has pushed or even barred exit or entry, one can be deemed a batterer. If one has grabbed the other's forearm, say, or wrist, or shoulder—and further, that such an event is a single occurrence with no precedent and no recurrence or escalation in the future—that individual may still be labeled *batterer* or *abusive*. Can we not all imagine intersubjective and otherwise interpersonal situations when such labels may or may not be applicable, and in which more information is needed with which to make a determination?

Hitting, kicking, and biting are obviously abusive behaviors. Right? Well, there are ambiguous areas even in these grosser actions. I am thinking of a violent six-year-old boy, Willy, placed in a psychiatric hospital ninety miles from his hometown, where he stayed for a year. He was indeed violent, and his behavior was unequivocally difficult to manage, but only the whys and wherefores of his violence told the whole story. His mother, Johnnie, was extremely narcissistic, cyclothymic, and impinged on her son's efforts at idiomatic elaboration. He was instead expected to remain within narrow behavioral, emotional, and attitudinal parameters, such that he conformed to the external needs of whatever his mother's exigent psychic state of the moment happened to be. Ordinary and innocuous requests by him were often capriciously denied. He was periodically "backhanded" or slapped in ways that must have felt to him like being descended upon by some *diabolus ex machina*. He sometimes had his mouth "washed out" with soap or cayenne sauce poured on his tongue. Sometimes his violence was in direct response to his mother's transgressions, sometimes it was not. He could at times strike out forcefully, with impunity, and with no concern whatsoever for the other. He could attack his younger and quite defenseless sister with little or no provocation on her part. But when do we "hold him accountable?" Is he abusive based solely on his effect upon the other? Do we consider the inner and outer world he is made to live in when we decide whether to invoke the signifier *abuse*? Is he deemed abusive as a six year old at those times when we can see that he clearly is a child, blinded by overwhelming inner processing of some event? Is it easier for us to consider such a question with a child, especially the younger he is? Witness our dilemmas over prosecuting juveniles for corporeal crimes; we have no such dilemma for an eighteen-year-old boy. But what makes him no longer a juvenile? Does age actually render the "offender" more culpable, or does his greater age merely conceal our culpability for a retaliatory justice? If so, small concealment, for it is obvious that there is no line of demarcation for accountability capacity that occurs from one year to the next, indeed from one day to the next, as one enters the date upon which our laws designate prosecutability as an adult, complete with the death sentence in certain circumstances.

Now, an example very different from our six year old—one sure to cause a bit of consternation here and there. Imagine Harry, an engineer of some renown, who is a meek man in many respects, but perhaps especially when he must deal with the volatile affective expulsions of Bonnie, his borderline wife. She harangues him rather ruthlessly and in an ongoing stream of redundant criticisms of his character; and she does this not only in a relatively unilateral communication to him but also around town, indiscriminately telling people that she is so terribly aggrieved and long-suffering, having to abide her husband's purported latent schizophrenia. He is far from schizophrenic and quite understands the humiliation she is laying him open to with such public recitations. For his part, he *is* an obsessional, terribly passive-aggressive, and astutely skilled in that art; he is no innocent in the battle of the psyches. But . . . she *is* very difficult, and his usual way of responding to her harangues is to try to reason with her, or else to pepper her with underhandedness. His more efficacious hostilities are enacted in more surreptitious venues than in her open field of affective display. So at times such as these, he is at a decided disadvantage. In the heat of one such outburst, he felt himself cross some subjective line and be struck with the vision of bodily picking her up, carrying her out the door, and dropping her into the snowbank. Which he did!

In the process, with her vehemently and indignantly resisting, she banged her shin hard against a handrail—enough to "leave a mark." She called the police, and he was arrested for domestic violence. How clear is it to refer to this action on his part as abuse? It was so prosecuted. He spent a few days in jail. To my mind, we are on thin ice to approach this clinically from an angle that is victimological. In that case, we are compelled to see him as abusive, with no commentary on the possibility of concomitant abusiveness by her. He was labeled a batterer, whether by the battered women's shelter or instead by Bonnie's misapprehension of the shelter's vernacular. The term *batterer* became a part of Bonnie's linguistic arsenal, invoking this designation when she wanted to control or belittle him. Whereas the case of our six year old, above, constitutes an overassignment of abuse, this one occupies an erroneous space ofdissemblingly unilateral assignation. And, indeed, it may be an overassignation in the first place.

Let's use the above example as well with which to cite an underassignation of abuse. That is, by the definition I believe we must clinically consider, there is the possibility, when deciding whether or not to categorize actions as abusive, that such actions as Bonnie's haranguings of the spouse above would have to be construed as abusive. Why I say so will soon become evident.

Or imagine a sternly intoned reprimand or warning to one's child. The same message, listened to by two different people, might be considered either setting a firm limit where called for, or instead a mordant evacuation of the speaker's psychic state.

In any event, "abuse" labelings are often used in dehumanizing, pseudospeciating ways, rendering the labeled something nonhuman, rather like wartime epithets designed to make killing one's enemy seem not like an act of murdering a fellow human being. Our uses of "He's a batterer!"

cating the constituents of abuse place us in a *no man's land* of nosological false-negatives and false-positives. Rather, we must look below the surface, within the interior if we are to understand whether a thing is abusive or traumatic. While the women's rights movement is creditable with our advances in awareness of abuses of power differentials, to continue to look at abuse victimologically may be "politically correct" in some quarters but it is woefully insufficient clinically.

I suggest that when attempting to categorize a thing or person as abusive, we must consider both conscious and unconscious intent or communication of the subject, as well as the inner experiences of the object of possible abuse. In that vein, I suggest that abuse is the ego-defensive use of interaction or communication which 1. is consciously or unconsciously traumatic for the recipient—that is, an overt behavior in and of itself could not be categorized as abusive; 2. defensively blames the recipient for the activation in the subject of the subject's own intolerable and uncontainable psychic state; and 3. includes the subject's induction in the recipient of these defended-against states.[3] Last, and though I do not feel justified to make any definitional addendum with this comment, I can say that in order to understand the meaning of the subject's potentially abusive behavior, we must consider 4. the interpersonal, intersubjective context in which it arose.[4] That is, we must apply at least the above three questions to our considerations of the recipient, and attempt to grasp what the subject might not have been able to contain, arguably due to his own shortcomings but not thereby unworthy of consideration, of what the recipient had expelled into them.

Willy, our six year old above, is in a bit of an ambiguous signifying space here. His behavior could often indeed be traumatic for its recipient. He at times blamed the recipient for an inner state of his own. And he would also at times induce the other to experience his warded-off psychic states. However, his psychic state was indeed quite directly precipitated and cumulatively derived from his mother's gross mishandling of him, as well as at other times being so derived from his day treatment center's countertransference mismanagement (see chapter 6), thus yielding at least a partially iatrogenic reaction the center misconstrued as Willy's abusiveness.[5] Is this then abuse or not? And even if it is, which, if it met the three criteria I have set forth, would have to be considered the case, we are still clinically bound to ascertain the context in which the abuse took place, or else we have quite failed to grasp its meaning and are blaming, erroneously assigning signification through too simplistic and unilateral a locating of source: "He did it, so he is out of control." In part 3, on treatment I will go

or "He's so abusive!" are often utterred in this fashion. "Wife-beater" is especially incisive in this regard. Bettelheim (1974), in discussing severely disturbed children, cautioned his readers thus: "The message of this book will be lost on the reader who permits himself to think of "patients" as one class of people and "therapists" as another. These two terms refer to people who are very much individuals, with their own life histories and personalities, but who are also in many respects very much like the rest of us, the author and the reader" (8). Cindy Garthwaite, a social work professor at the University of Montana, once told an audience at a child abuse seminar that we are disposed to think of abusive parents as one group and of nonabusive parents as another, but that although such dichotomizing may be comforting it is also misguided. My point is simply that we need to break out of facile categorical comfortings and examine abuse in a light which honors a bit of the complexity, ambiguity, and foundational primitivity of human nature.

DEFINITIONS

The *Oxford English Dictionary* tells us that *abuse* is derived from the Latin *abusare*, to use up, misuse, or disuse, and variously defines it as "to use improperly, to ill-use or maltreat; to injure, wrong, or hurt; to wrong with words, to speak injuriously of or to; to malign." Its noun form includes such additional defining characteristics as "misapplication. . . injury. . . injurious speech . . . abusive language." It is of no small parenthetical relevance to note the obvious point this definition raises: to wrongly apply such signifiers as *abusive* or *batterer* to an individual is itself abusive. The *OED* indicates that *trauma* is derived from the Greek *wound* and is defined as a wound or external bodily injury in general, also the condition caused by this;" and as "*Psychoanalysis* and *Psychiatry*. A psychic injury, especially one caused by emotional shock the memory of which is repressed and remains unhealed." We seem to use both terms synonymously and as an amalgamation of the two. And clearly our application to nonphysical realms of the infliction and suffering of abuse and trauma are consistent with the *OED*'s. It is in these senses that I too am using the terms. However, just as the DSM-III and its successors are criticized as being more political documents than clinical ones, due to their overt and description-observable litanizing of diagnostic criteria without reliance upon an underlying personality theory frame of reference, so do I think our relying on observable data for lo-

into some detail about two abusive adolescents whose violent acting-out against staff in previous treatment centers, though it stretched then existing staff resources, did not materialize at Constancy House for the one year of its operation, that behavior partly due to our not having iatrogenically created it.

Harry: when he carried his wife to and dropped her into the snowbank, did his actions meet the criterion of inducing in his wife that which he could not then tolerate internally? Probably.[6] But to grasp his dynamic and structural reactions, don't we need to know the intersubjective context of his behavior's origins? What projective identifications were deployed? What introjective counteridentifications occurred? Was his wife abusive? Was she unconsciously projecting into him mental contents or ego states that she could not bear? If they existed, how forceful were her evacuations? How forcefully might she have tried to manipulate him for him to experience a disruptive inner state? Did Harry try to contain her evacuations? Was his failure to contain them a dovetailing with his own repudiated needs? Doesn't he need to know something of these questions himself? Not to mention some of the answers!

Of Harry and Bonnie, was one of them morally or ethically more reasonably prosecution-worthy than the other? Probably not. But only he was arrested. And if we accept the facts as presented, which we may easily do for argument's sake, inasmuch as they are conceivable, Bonnie was the more volatile and Harry was the more psychically aggrieved in that situation. If, clinically, we ipso facto accept the event and dynamic rendering of which Harry's adjudicated guilt informs us, we will be blind and will proceed accordingly.

WHEN THE SYSTEM GOES AWRY

In this section, I argue that allied professionals, including shelter staff, victims' rights advocates, batterer and victim therapists, prosecutors, and child protection workers are all subject to either consciously or unconsciously conveying information in counterproductive ways, or, and I believe and hope that the latter is the case, are at risk of having their communications misconstrued and appropriated. And, in the latter case, being sensitized to these pitfalls might help to circumvent them, while, even in the former case, having them named may nascently offset them through the development of a new linguistically sponsored viewscape.

I will further add that I anticipate two objections, as I have not uncommonly already been met with these reactions. One will be, "Doesn't the author think that professionals already realize this?" I most decidedly do not think so, and, in my opinion, it is too facile a dismissal and reprieve from the self-examination demands these views place upon us to assume that they are so obvious as not to need stating. Conversely, and ironically, an objection will be made that I am either suggesting that men ought to be exculpated for their violent enactments whenever anything like provocation exists: I hope it is obvious to most readers that this is simply not a view I have, nor does it stand to reason that because one felt, or was, provoked he can then justify the *law of talion*. We merely want to consider as much information as we are able to, in the hope of making informed clinical and supportive interventions.

Let's take the case of Helen and Hector. Their case may or may not be a representative one, but I fear that it is. Helen was not differentially diagnosed, but I do know that she was either an hysteric or a borderline. Neither was Hector's diagnosis differentiated; he appeared alternately to be narcissistic, impulse-neurotic, and depressed, borderline, or psychopathic.[7] I saw them both only briefly, as they became embroiled in the vicissitudes of the victims' rights network and I did not then have the analytic aplomb and equanimity to hold them both in an analytic space in which they could feel conscious or unconscious asylum from the networking body of providers.[8] Whether my relative maturity would now suffice is a matter worth speculating about.

Helen made her first call to 911 when Hector would not let her walk out from a fight they were having. Presumably, they were both in the midst of intolerable affective and mental states that each was trying to evacuate into the other. Presumably, their argument was punctuated by a number of reasonable arguments and entreaties by one to the other, with little moments of hope of feeling heard quickly deteriorating, new evacuations ensuing. However we might diagnose them, it was clear that they were both "screamers," each able to yell and otherwise spout all sorts of vitriol.

When Helen got a chance to call the police, they sent a squad car out, and determined that they could not make an arrest merely on her report that Hector detained her. But they did offer to give her and the couple's two children a ride to the battered women's shelter. And that was the beginning of Helen's longstanding relationship with the shelter. She found the staff's standard rhetoric about women's and victim's rights invigorating, even mesmerizing; indeed, it became a battle cry for her. She would oscillate between it and passionate reunions with Hector. Indeed, over time the shelter staff grew very frustrated with Helen's resolutions to stay away from Hector, which were followed by inevitable returns. When she was in a frame of mind in which Hector was to be villainized, she found the shelter and its rhetoric, or was it rather her misapprehension and appropriation of it? fuel for her defensive blaming. Any consideration of her own disavowed self states as contributing to the battles between her and Hector were easily rationalized.[9] She began to flee to the shelter more regularly, and Hector's violence escalated. But was Helen fleeing because Hector's violence was escalating, or was Hector's violence escalating in helpless response to an unthought but known surrendering of Helen to the shelter, which Hector experienced as taking his wife from him? Concomitantly, Helen's mounting mental arsenal, replete with simplistic and at times defensive allegations of his "power and control" tactics and motives, were beyond Hector's capacity to detoxify, and he found himself thrust more and more upon desperate defenses against disintegration anxiety. His dependency needs were being squashed, and the resurrection of unthought-known childhood abandonment constituted a conservative object that Hector could not resist.

Bonnie, too, found her way to the shelter, and quite often. She used it as a haven when she and Harry argued, though there were never further instances of corporal conflict resolution. She too adopted the shelter's rhetoric, and often used it to harangue Harry. This was a flawed apprehension of the shelter's mission statement, and an appropriation of it for her own defensive purposes.

Considerations of the complexity and often inherently obfuscatory nature of intimate violence and of what constitutes abuse would allow for conceptual checks and balances against this type of misuse of not only shelters but also the domestic violence network of professionals in general, as they set about their extremely difficult tasks.

What I imagine is the most common scenario in the stagings of intimate violence is that both spouses enter a spiraling succession of progressively abusive handlings of each other, and one or the other becomes violent first, or only one or the other becomes violent at all. In the latter event, it may be either spouse who becomes violent or strikes the first blow. But to characterize one party as a perpetrator and the other as a victim in such a situation is a specious critical tack. Why do we navigate so blindly and so confidently? That will be my subject in the next chapter.

CHAPTER FIVE

OUR UNWITTING PERSECUTION OF THE BATTERER AND OTHER FACILE CONVENIENCES

Our country's efforts in the last couple of decades to raise social consciousness about domestic violence, while successful in that immediate aim, have yielded some disturbing, destructive, and pervasive consequences. Perhaps most egregrious, we have tended to perceive batterers as only men hitting women, too often recognizing with a split-off and unintegrated awareness that, for example, male and female homosexual partners are sometimes violent with each other, both fathers and mothers violently abuse their children, and wives sometimes hit their husbands for the same reasons that husbands sometimes hit their wives. We have tragically erred in adopting a monothetic depiction of "the batterer," when careful clinical study shows that only an idiographic frame of reference is germane, the latter requiring us to form perceptions of each domestically violent and battered individual based on his or her inherent human singularity and complexity. Batterers and victims both cover wide ranges of psychological strengths and weaknesses. And they occupy positions of infinite diversity pursuant to pathognomonic intrapsychic conflict.

In many states we have formed legislative, prosecutorial, police, and therapist responses to domestic violence that monothetically perceive "the batterer" in dramatically heinous ways and act to impart messages to the falsely dichotomized "victim" that she would be better off away from her villainous husband,[1] and any complementary psychological problems she carries herself are subsumed under such hackneyed rubrics as "codependency," often translated to the battered woman as, "Your only problem is that you stay with that man."[2] Psychotherapists have often split, forming specialties of treating either victims or batterers, tending to avoid or even dismiss efforts at couples therapy, even denigrating therapists who offer such a service. Battered women's shelters are typically characterized by similarly false dichotomies. Courts grant temporary restraining orders, sometimes effectively criminalizing the couple's enacting of any conjoint therapy. Psychotherapy of either spouse is often, at least in part, a kind of cajoling or entreating of the patient to accept these persecutory views. Additionally, the typical psychotherapies are brief, consonant with "managed-care" mandates and our fast-food, immediate gratification culture, leaving patients to founder in the aftermath of these cajolings when treatment has ended. Psychoanalytic psychotherapists, who are trained to know better, may either not wish to work with these patients because of their intractability or may not recognize when these patients are in their practices, the violence going unreported by the patient and unconsidered by the therapist.

There is a stark paucity of willing psychotherapists who know enough and are themselves analyzed at all, or well-enough analyzed (in their own personal analyses), to have much of a chance at providing deeply adequate treatment for any and all members of domestically violent families. Instead, our collective system denies the possible existence of pathological ego defenses in one spouse, while humiliating and threatening the other, unwittingly causing him a greater need for his pathological defenses. This easily yields, in a self-fulfilling prophetic manner, an individual who, in response to these systemic transgressions, appears all the more to be the very thing he was accused of.

Over one hundred years ago Freud, in his and Breuer's *Studies on Hysteria* (1895), was already writing of the folly of mere psychoeducational and suggestive efforts in the absence of psychic work. He showed that a sine qua non for the acquisition of psychoneuroses was "an incompatibility should develop between the ego and some idea presented to it" (122). Though he was discussing hysteria, the similarities to other conditions is obvious against the backdrop of considerations we have been discussing in this book. He was addressing trauma and the self's struggle with it. "The actual traumatic moment, then, is the one at which the incompatibility forces itself upon the ego and at which the latter decides on the repudiation of the incompatible idea. That idea is not annihilated by a repudiation of this kind, but merely repressed into the unconscious" (123). It is only "in compelling the psychical group that had been split off to unite once more with the ego-consciousness" (124) that any treatment success becomes possible. The affects attendant to the original traumata had to be abreacted, or else all other interventions were doomed to yield only temporary results or a substitution of the presenting symptoms with yet new ones. Still, we expect a batterer, who has endured and split off a good deal of trauma, to achieve treatment success without benefit of such work. We do not consider that our blamings, our premature interpretations, our systemically enacted humiliations, such as arrests and incarcerations, or our gross impingements upon batterers' narcissistic equilibria by imposing court-mandated group treatment whose hours may require conflicts in sometimes already strained relations with employers, not to mention loss of income that these patients often can ill afford—we do not consider that our actions may often be causing further harm, not to mention that our actions are so often only scratching the surface. Or what of the impact when a patient goes through a short-term program—with its implication that now he ought to be able to manage his behavior—and he finds that he cannot? What is he left with?

Essentially, the system tends to drive a psychological wedge between spouses, or even to drop a psychological hammer on these families. Yet many of these couples and families want to stay together, and many are treatable, given sophisticated and lengthy enough treatment. Both spouses often have tendencies to blame each other incorrectly for intolerable subjective experiences that culminate in battering and its nonphysical concomitants. A system that only perceives these blaming tendencies in the designated batterer is often feeding the vicious cycle of intolerable subjective helplessness that leads to battering. That is, the system ends up being a mirror of some of the same pathological defenses and original pathogenic experiences found in both batterer and victim. In fact, for those batterers and victims who cycle again and again through this system, how much are they unconsciously resonating to a resurrection of the pathologies in their families of origin, be it a libidinized privation, or humiliation, or triangulation, or what have you? Mightn't they be finding themselves on the same kind of familiar and paradoxically longed for turf of libidinized pathogenesis, much like boys and men who find homes of a sort in reform schools and penitentiaries?[3]

Just as with their families, which killed off intrapsychic complexity and consideration and instead insisted upon false self adjustment, this system (federal and state legislatures,[4] judges, prosecutors, therapists, shelters), in varying component combinations, denies the validity of systemic, depth-psychological, and idiographic frames of reference. It splits off the "bad man" and the "good woman," blames the bad man for being a cruel, calloused, childlike, and thoughtless fiend to the good woman. (Of course, this is also grossly infantilizing to the woman in such a scenario, is it not?

when she is consequently, though unwittingly, treated as someone with no capacity to look at matters of interiority herself.) The system provides interventions doomed to fail, while later blaming the batterer for failed treatment and the victim for foolishly, or "innocently," staying with "him." Such superego actings-out thus hurled by the system do great and pervasive damage. While the system's perpetrators are busy distancing themselves, in their conscious self-representations, from the abusive, impulsive tendencies in all of us, while this system self-righteously calumniates patients under the guises of justice and psychotherapeutic intervention, many families are being needlessly torn apart, in the service of the pathological defenses of this system's perpetrators. The tendencies to witch-hunt are obfuscating and undermining the system's accomplishments of courageous perception, and transmission of same to society's consciousness, of real physical and psychological dangers, in all their bewildering complexities, present in domestically violent families. There, wives are being encouraged to see their husbands' problems as both sole representatives of who these men are and to see the violence and its concomitants as the only problem in a marital relationship that is no less complicated by the existence of intimate violence. With such an inculcated frame of reference in the wife, to the degree she identifies with it, she cannot help but be blaming and denigrating of her spouse, without noticing this thrust of her action and attitudes.[5]

Men, women, and couples do sometimes leave violence behind. Children sometimes do discover changing parents who become capable of noticing their traumatizations of their children and developing the impulse control to cease an intergenerational transmission of violence. Parents do sometimes courageously confront their unwittingly and defensively destructive behavior. These patients can change. Unfortunately, the same system that gratefully brought to our attention so much about the existence and consequences of domestic violence is now predictably, given its humanity, mired in its own systemic pathologies. Therefore, I am following the courageous example of feminist and consciousness-raising pioneers and naming the problem and its consequences.

This system, like its predeceased oppressor, is in something of a position of political power, and is also similarly able to invoke its innocence, an innocence that, as I have argued, is capable of yielding violence: to families, to individuals, to either spouse, to children.[6]

PART 3

TREATMENT

CHAPTER SIX

COUNTERTRANSFERENCE

In order to examine the batterer's transference needs with open minds, we must first attend to our own countertransference resistances: there are good reasons many clinicians do not want to or cannot work with batterers.[1]

Our current state of grappling with legitimate feminist concerns still finds us largely identifying with the perceived oppressed and villainizing the perceived oppressor, a state of affairs that is further fueled by our free-standing witch-hunting propensities, the latter of which may exist in all of us to some extent, at least as a potential. Certainly as a mass body, the propensity is strong and easily actualized in the *herd* or in our fear of naming and speaking aloud the herd's injustices. So it is that I believe, as addressed in chapter 5, our preexisting societywide projective, tendencies to villify have partially co-opted the legitimate feminist-initiated fight against spouse abuse, and therein bastardized it into its utility as a container for our disavowed abusive self components. We have acquired a convenient recipient for our shadow projections in "the batterer." A victimology approach lends itself well to this purpose, as we then systemically designate and diametrically oppose the duality of a batterer-victim pair. This leads us into hallucinatorily clear waters wherein the patient is criminalized and easily made into the villain. One is reminded again of Aichhorn's (1948) and Eissler's (1949) warnings and injunctions (see introduction).

This alone is a strong pitfall for the therapist, but it is potentiated by still further salient and powerful factors. There are tremendous problems working with narcissistic patients in general, of whom batterers are merely one subset, narcissistic pathology being so difficult for therapists that Freud was moved to refer to these patients' resistances as "the stone wall of narcissism," deeming this class of patients "unanalyzable." Morever, to these issues may be added the specific self- and other-annihilating senses that batterers may induce in therapists who work closely with them. The yield of this redoubtable set of factors is that of a countertransference that is an amalgam of individually difficult resistances.

To do effective work with these patients requires the successful negotiation of these treacherous waters, again and again. Yet, at the same time, in one form or another, we may come across these factors in all thoroughgoing treatment cases. Just as Spotnitz's pioneering work with schizophrenics ultimately allowed for the illumination of the ubiquity of the narcissistic defense, i.e., that it is to be found to some degree in all analyses, I wonder if identification with the aggressor may not be found to exert its presence in all analyses, in both patients and their analysts. That is, our counterresistances to being aware of our inductions to mistreat our patients, in actually abusive ways, pursuant to the defense of identification with the aggressor, may be a ubiquitous factor, one that rears its head in every analysis, made observable only to the degree that we successfully grapple with it. And, more to the point, this is a character counterresistance in therapists, who must become well acquainted with both their hostile propensities and their idiomatic character resistances to observing them.

Robert and Simone Marshall (1988) begin their chapter on countertransference with the following quote by Hanna Segal (1977), which, in its brevity, speaks volumes: "Countertransference is the best of servants, but the worst of masters." It is a tool that, when used well, is invaluable, but that, when misused or unnoticed, can be terribly destructive. And all the more so, the more potent the psychopathology with which we are dealing.

HISTORICAL PERSPECTIVE ON THE CONCEPT

Before proceeding further, however, some of the historical evolution of the concept of countertransference deserves enunciation. Initially seen as an impediment to treatment, the analyst experiencing countertransference was thought to be in need of reparative self-analysis, or even of returning to his own personal analyst in order to resolve the problem. For the analyst, signs of countertransference often carried insulting implications of ill-health.

Gradually, it was recognized that countertransference was unavoidable, but it was still considered undesirable and unhelpful. It was not until the 1950s that it became acceptable to begin considering it both inevitable *and* potentially very useful. We have come to consider countertransference as one side of a coin, transference and countertransference being the outcrop of each unique therapist-patient dyad. No patient would experience exactly the same transference with different analysts, and various analysts necessarily provide their own idiomatic countertransferences with respective patients. But it is always within this "dialogue" of the transference-countertransference matrix that treatment takes place (Marshall and Marshall 1988). Robert Marshall emphasized that point in the following.

> Every patient seeks to recreate the troublesome past while seeking to avoid it. Every patient studies the therapist to determine whether or not the therapist can be helpful. What seems to keep patients in treatment is their idea that *at the same time* they can work maximally toward recreating and resolving past developmental failures and conflicts while minimizing the hurt from affects that attended the earlier maturational failure (1982:49).

This subtly profound statement is easy to underemphasize, periodically, in our practices. But we do so at the peril of our patients as well as of ourselves.

At this point, then, let me offer a working definition of countertransference, one that will serve to facilitate its examination here. Countertransference is the conscious and unconscious inner response of the analyst to the patient's transference; moreover, and especially, it is the transference-induced or evoked analyst experiences that interface with the patient's experiences in such a manner that we are brought (carried by the force of the relationship) to a juncture that will replicate some aspect(s) of the patient's healthful or unhealthful formative registration and lived sense of earlier self-other events.[2] We are thus placed in the position of being scanned, so to speak, for our similarity or dissimilarity to the patient's registration of formative, original others. When these situations are pursuant to original pathogenic experiences, we are placed in the position of either reenacting original pathogenic perceived events, or of giving the patient transformational experiences, corrective emotional experiences,[3] or experiences which serve to offset, compensate for, or in some other way give new templates to the patient for further, new, and healthy self and other experiences. This definition focuses on objective countertransference (Winnicott 1947), as opposed to subjective (Spotnitz 1985) or therapist-induced countertransference (Marshall and Marshall 1988).

Subjective countertransference would be those countertransference responses which are a function of the therapist's own character, would not be expected to be elicited universally, and is generally considered to be attributable to unanalyzed defensive structures in the therapist. "Feelings that the therapist developed for persons who were emotionally significant to him early in life are revived by the patient's symbolic recapitulation of his own childhood experience in the analytic situation. . . any tendency to communicate the therapist's subjective reactions impulsively to the patient, whether verbally or in behavior, needs to be recognized and mastered" (Spotnitz 1985:229).[4] Conversely, objective countertransference is a function of what Ogden (1982:71) called "mature reactions to the realistically perceived current situation."

COUNTERRESISTANT, PROJECTIVE MISUSE OF LEGITIMATE HUMANITARIAN AND FEMINIST CONCERNS

Due largely or predominantly to feminist consciousness, we have developed an awareness of the absurd and atrocious use of power and control, by men over women, through the use of or augmented by battering. The days in which spousal violence by the husband were condoned, through lack of existence or of implementation of legal sanction, are largely behind us. The exercise of his typically greater strength in the man's wish to "have things his way" over or with a woman is no longer acccepted or ignored by our society. Interspousal terror and violence are legally prohibited, punishable, and punished. Legislative prohibition against domestic violence has allowed muscle to battering consciousness raising.[5] However, the domestic violence intervention field, and child protective services for that matter, stand to gain much by being informed by psychoanalysis. The type of issues discussed in part 2 make it difficult for us to embrace a complex and multifactoral conceptualization. It is tempting to embrace a view of "He simply must stop!" Prevailing models of batterer intervention, with the inchoate exceptions I have mentioned, have unwittingly embraced too simplistic a truth, have eschewed psychodynamic and psychostructural considerations. In the spirit of Jane Flax's *Thinking Fragments: Psychoanalysis, Feminism, and Postmodernism in the Contemporary West* (1990), I suggest that in domestic violence concerns, we must integrate the following. We must simultaneously recognize

1. the power and control motives of spousal violence and emotional abuse (ditto in regard to corporal punishment);

2. that, conversely, there are subjectively threatening unconscious and deeply disruptive internal experiences being defended against by any abusive individual and therefore,in order to be of substantive assistance, we will need to take these less observable but important factors into consideration;

3. *and keep as a consideration in our theory building and in case conceptualizing* that domestic violence and other forms of domestic abuse occur not only by men against women, but also by women against men, both genders against children,and homosexual lovers against each other;[6]

4. while criminalization of domestic violence is helpful in some regards, it concomitantly lends itself well to our projective tendencies to locate "monsters" outside of ourselves and the resultant villainization of the batterer as the Neanderthalic, sadism-loving, demonized wife-beater popularized in numerous recent movies and documentaries and many contemporary intervention programs to which batterers are referred under threat of incarceration.

Under the influence of popular factors without balance from depth factors, it becomes difficult to think of one's batterer patient as a struggling human being in need of assistance. Instead, we are invited to think he is someone who needs to be "put in his place," confronted with "who he *really* is," controlled by the system so that he cannot abuse again. I recall Carl Whitaker telling an audience of several hundred in Bozeman, Montana about a decade ago that the so-called reporting laws were inconsonant with and destructive to the function and name of the therapist, that they required us to be policemen rather than therapists. Many in the audience took horrified and vehement exception to this view; we resist this mightily. Or consider Bollas and Sundelson's *The New Informants: The Betrayal of Confidentiality in Psychoanalysis and Psychotherapy*, in which a strong and unequivocal case is made for depth-oriented therapists, at the least to recover lost ground and attend to our having collegially agreed to relinquish *privilege*, rather like that protected by other professions such as the clergy, journalists, and attorneys. *We have literally rewritten codes of ethics in order to allow us to "ethically" and legally give information to managed care companies that would have been impossible under the older codifications.* These authors also make a distressingly compelling argument for the importance to depth treatment of a confidentiality that would never allow us to cooperate with such laws as the *duty to warn* and *child abuse and neglect*. However, these laws go quite unchallenged and are in fact at times not only cooperated with but used as implements of coercion or retaliation by unwitting therapists against patients, of course under the guise of good patient care ("for your own good") or moral rectitude.

To the extent that we believe, *consciously or unconsciously*, that the patient must be controlled, we will be unable to establish ourselves, within their *conscious and unconscious minds*, as professionals that can be potentially helpful to them. As Bollas and Sundelson point out, even if the patient gives us permission to *violate his confidentiality*, it is solely his conscious mind giving this permission, as the unconscious mind is therein inaccessible for consultation. Therapists who accept court-ordered cases must keep in mind that the patient will arrive at our doors having often felt humiliated by the "system," and, in addition, associating us unconsciously or consciously, with this same system. The court or the prosecutor, depending on where one practices, may expect to have access to the patient's perceived degree of "cooperation with treatment." I believe therapists are unconsciously (countertransferentially or even transferentially) embracing of such an idea, inasmuch as it gives them a venue for acting out against difficult patients (who may often be difficult more iatrogenically than otherwise), since it is easily deployable as an implied or stated threat when patients fail to comply with a certain false self accommodating to therapists.[7] Rather than having patients sign a release of information that allows for such disclosures, releases instead could be made only to cover the disclosure to prosecutor or court of what the patient's attendance is. If a patient cannot behave in a manner viable for treatment, he does not belong in the group. Thus such a patient can be barred from the treatment setting, and the therapist will need to inform the authorities why the patient is being discharged; a release of information may allow for such a potentiality. But if a patient is to be a patient rather than one incarcerated, he must be free to speak his mind without fear of reprisal.

Puck is a great case in point of the patient whose acting-in (i.e., defensively using acting in the transference rather than transformative wording) may have been more an iatrogenic than a self manifestation. He had to be physically restrained on numerous treatment occasions before and after his one year at Constancy House, but never *at* Constancy House itself. Not that it wouldn't have been easy to give in to the frightening aspects of his identifications with his abusive stepfather and a mother who repeatedly appropriated his transitional space, harshly denigrating him in ways that simultaneously insisted that he consciously register her cruelty as a kind of exciting affection. These were curious events to be witness to. After not seeing him for months, having been off on a spree of one sort or another, she would, for example, insult some new adornment or valued idea of his, which hepresented to her proudly. Once he was showing off a new haircut, which he felt made him look more grown up. She said, "Oh, that's so silly. That makes you look like one of those little sissy boys we used to laugh at in the old neighborhood, right?!" And she roughed his hair and punched him in the arm so that he knew he was meant to indicate agreement with her and enjoyment of what she'd just said and done.

His abusive stepfather violently beat the boy on numerous occasions, and while Puck resented him and even blamed him for the state's termination of his mother's parental rights, Puck was far more like John than he could have imagined.

When Puck entered into behavioral conflicts with the staff at Constancy House, he had an uncanny way of deploying projective identifications that embodied both of his parents' powers and woundings of him. He would easily, with no guilt or no recognition, mistreat a fellow resident or staff member and insist that he was merely being playful and, What the hell was our problem that we couldn't see that, anyway! He would become very intimidating toward anyone who stood in his way whenever he was busy evacuating difficult self experiences.

Once, when I arrived late at a group therapy meeting, he was hiding under a blanket, like a little boy. However, I soon learned from others present that he had scared the hell out of both another resident and a staff member when he was asked to turn off the TV for group session. He had begun to yell and insisted he was about to turn off the fucking TV when someone else turned it off instead! When he was told that he was frightening, he curiously disappeared under the blanket. But the fear remained in the room. When I arrived, that's where he was, and when a staff member tried to get him to come out from under the blanket, he yelled threateningly, "If you don't leave me the fuck alone, you're gonna see real trouble!"

I judged that this impasse had to be broken, that it was not going to clear up spontaneously. I knew that he was feeling trapped, but that he was intent on evacuating this experience. To merely have given the option of removing the blanket and talking, or of having it removed for him, would clearly have led immediately into a violent altercation. I sat right next to

him, told him that the blanket had to come off and why, how he was affecting people, that this was exactly the kind of situation that had often
eventuated in restraint, that I knew we were (residents and staff) feeling
much of what he did not want to remember or register of how he felt and
indeed sometimes still feels with his mother and stepfather, that I was
going to take the blanket off him, and that we were going to talk rather
than have an event. He was by then becoming accessible, but it remained
a bit unclear what would happen. I had to trust that my grasp of the situation and the way I conveyed it to him had sufficiently reached the boy
who needed mirroring. I did remove the blanket and he began to cry,
telling us all how he had been beaten on a number of occasions and how
his mother had acted like only a little wimp would think anything of it. He
was deeply hurt, and the fear that we all had felt a few minutes ago seemed
a distant memory, as a real live boy now sat before us.

But we all had had to contain his intrusion of himself into the real, his
imposing of actual trauma that could not simply be dealt with by talking,
as he made sure to keep us all in fear. We had to know that this was a re-
visitation of his ghosts he was attempting to give to us. And it was easy to
see why. We didn't want them any more than he did.

This sort of thing would happen at his alternative school, or at a day
treatment center before that, and he was either restrained, or the police
were called, or the group home staff were called. Though not having to be
restrained even once during my tenure at Constancy House, he went on to
be restrained over and over again in two psychiatric placements after his
decline upon my departure.

The larger societal forces at work with a patient like Puck tell us that we
ought to set firm limits if Puck or his fellow residents are to feel safe. We
are not expected to grapple with his inner world, but are expected to make
him grapple with it alone. In a victimology-guided approach, he is simply
supposed to comply, and *then and only then* will anyone attempt to treat
him with dignity. Before that, society at large "tells" therapists to see him
as a threat who should not be coddled, not allowed to get away with such
bullying. In fact, curiously intelligent without knowing it or stepping up to
the plate of such knowledge, is the societal adage "Don't take any shit off
them!" It is in fact a kind of anal-sadistic evacuation that is occurring, by
both the patient and then the therapist or staff in such actings—in the
transference and the countertransference, in which both are manipulating
each other to take or to take back unwanted mental contents.

SOME COMMON COUNTERTRANSFERENCE RESISTANCES IN THE TREATMENT OF CHARACTER AND BEHAVIOR PATHOLOGY

Factors discussed above are potentially treatment-destructive counterresistances, or sources thereof, that may impose themselves on the therapist even before there has been any contact with the patient. They are powerful but externally introduced factors that are not directly generated by the transference-countertransference situation but do potentially have great impact on it. In addition to these concerns, let us review general narcissistic resistances that are a function of the particular narcissistic, or pseudonarcissistic, patient we have chosen to call "the batterer." In this section I will present some of the struggles therapists must cognize when treating narcissistic patients.[8] In the next section I will address the manner in which these resistances and those addressed in the previous section are yet further potentiated by the specific countertransference resistances that our batterer patients bring to us.

NARCISSISTIC PATHOLOGY DEFINED

Before addressing common countertransference struggles encountered in work with narcissistic patients, I will explain my use of the term *narcissistic*. First, it should be clear that I am not referring to narcissistic personalities. I am referring to a much wider class of patients that includes narcissistic personalities. In the early days of psychoanalysis, *narcissistic neuroses* were differentiated from *psychoneuroses* or *transference neuroses*, the latter being the original subjects of psychoanalytic treatment, the former deemed *unanalyzable*. Freud's therapeutic work was understood to be most successful with hysterics and obsessive-compulsives. These were understood to be patients who were capable of establishing transferences, while narcissistic neurotic patients were seen as unable to. The modern psychoanalytic school has made pointed study of this and published a great deal about a *narcissistic transference*, while referring to the transferences of Freud's patients as being of the *object* variety. Object transferences are understood to be supported within a background of solid ego structure. The patients' ego functioning may well be impaired, but if they are object-transference-capable, then the impairment is a consequence of the solidly structured ego's being overwhelmed by disavowed psychic conflict. That is, psychoneurotic conflict, which can yield psychoses or pseudonarcissistic adjustments, occurs when the superego's dictates force the ego to repudiate id impulses perceived to be incompatible with an ego ideal.

These impulses were originally and popularly seen to arise from the oedipal situation. That is, the child's rivalry with the same-sex parent for the possession of the parent of the opposite sex was repressed because of the imagined threat of retaliation by the rival parent, or else by the child's wish not to alienate the valued same-sex parent by the child's effort to usurp the marital territory.

Moreover, Bollas (2000) has suggested that we might add to the hysteric's plight a wish to repudiate the genitality of the parents, which implies and brings along the loss of the pregenital maternal order, in which the child does not have to know of its lack of exclusivity with the mother. We are learning of additional ways of conceptualizing the vicissitudes of the oedipal struggles in other disorders as well.

It has been understood that psychoneurotic patients had reached an oedipal adjustment, although they might show signs of regression to earlier development. We realize that psychoneurotic patients have reasonable ego resources, have attained some reasonable measure of a sense of a *verbal self*, and have achieved a good measure of self-object differentiation, following Stern and Mahler respectively. Yet we also realize there may have been false self accommodations to environmental failures (to adequately meet the constitutional needs of a given child) that cause clinical pictures often to be easily mistakable as narcissistic pathology, owing to overt disorganization in the personality, but that these accommodations are underlied by a solid ego. Thus, hysterical psychoses are sometimes misunderstood as schizophrenias, a pseudonarcissistic batterer is misunderstood as character disordered, an obsessive compulsive is mistaken as a schizoid, ADHD and ADD children and adults, who might be agitated hysterics, are misdiagnosed and placed on medication, and, most commonly, volatile hysterics are mistaken for borderlines.

But disorders such as the major depressions, schizophrenias, severe character disorders, and childhood pervasive developmental disorders are all based upon an unstable foundation, an ego that is not solid and does not have strong resources. These are seen to arise out of disruptions in the preverbal or preoedipal sphere of development or existence—disruptions occurring in the original establishment of senses of emergent, core, and intersubjective self, or disturbances in any of the stages of Mahler's developmental schema. Psychopaths would fall into this group of patients, and it is of course this particular type that battered women and their advocates rightly fear, for these are often the charmers who may be able to appear to have healthy ego functioning. Our false positives occur in both directions when considering ego strength.

This preoedipal or preverbal group of patients is seen to internally occupy an earlier, innate narcissistic state, originally a primary hallucinatory stage of wish fulfillment, a stage of primary narcissism, in which it was not cognized by the infant that there is an other who attends to it or, later, that there is a third with whom one must share the second. Thus, as Klein taught us, the infant's innate aggression is turned against the mother in fantasy when it feels frustrated, without there being any conflict about it. At first, this lack of conflict is due to a sense of objectlessness, then to a sense of a primary split between the mother who is experienced as gratifying—the good mother—and the mother who is experienced as frustrating—the bad mother. The two are not related to as one being, so that aggression against the bad mother is not felt by the early infant as something that will be received by the good mother as well. In fact, it is the development of this recognition, the ushering in of *whole object relations*, that provides the capacity for empathy, loss, the wish to make reparation, depression. Thus this stage is called the *depressive position*, whereas its predecessor is called the *paranoid-schizoid position*.

We saw in the narcissistic neuroses that the ego had suffered disappointment at the hands of a loved or needed other to the extent that "the object-relationship was shattered. The result was not the normal one of a withdrawal of libido from its object and a displacement of it onto a new one, but something different. . . . It was withdrawn into the ego" (Freud 1917:586), yielding a secondary narcissism. Thereby, the patient's primary object choice becomes his own ego, making object transferences impossible—or, at least to the degree to which the withdrawal of libido inward is absolute, as any patient may oscillate between object and narcissistic transference states. To that extent, we can conceptualize thenarcissistic transference—a transference state unrecognized by Freud. Here lies the impotence of interpretations in the narcissistic neuroses, the source of there being "no one home," if you will, to receive them. We now know that these patients are treatable, but for them interpretation is not a reliable therapeutic tool, sometimes not for years. These are the disorders that appear clinically as Mahler described, as being unable to accept separateness and individuation in all its pleasurable and unpleasurable implications, disorders that defend against the discomfort of separateness/aloneness with the predominant defenses of splitting (of the good and bad part-objects) and the projection of disavowed aspects of self or other in order that unpleasant experiences may be evacuated. Here are disruptions in object constancy (Mahler), here are unstable senses of a core self (Stern). But foremost for our consideration, and so to reiterate, these are disorders that are not accessible to alteration via interpretation alone. Hence, for Freud, the stone wall.

NARCISSISTIC RESISTANCES

It is, in fact, narcissistic patients' inaccessibility through interpretation that accounts for a great deal of our countertransference struggles with them. We therein resist our feelings of helplessness when we seem to perceive "the problem" and believe we could solve it if only our patients could see the wisdom of our insight. However, so typically, the patient is either not interested in our interpretations or else profits from them little if at all. Or, we may see some narcissistic patients solve their presenting problems only to leave treatment precipitously, in comfort, consciously, while we are left with a knowledge they cannot see: they are still quite damaging to those dependent upon them.

Jacques was so enamored of his ability to make weaker persons suffer that there was no early dislodging of it possible. I had to accept his reflective inability to notice his evacuative maneuvers. Or perhaps it was more that he was not about to be interested in any meaningful analytic engagement about such cruelty, not when analytic engagement means the patient's wondering about his symptoms.

Winnicott (1971) spoke of the need to wait out such patients, avoiding the temptation to enjoy our own interpretations. What I have spoken of earlier as object transference entails the patient's ability "to use the analyst" (87), but many patients do not have this ability, and certainly most batterer patients do not. For Winnicott this meant that it must not be assumed that the patient is able to do more than "relate" to the object, that they are capable of seeing the object as "real in the sense of being part of shared reality, not a bundle of projections." "An acceptance of the object's independent existence" by the subject is not to be taken for granted. Yet it is such an assumption that underlies much of the cognitive and psychoeducational methods. Like the modern analysts after him, Winnicott was aware that there are necessary areas of the work, with many patients, that is preinterpretive, and that must involve certain attacks. A comment by one of my teachers comes to mind, "One of the most important things we can do for our children is to survive their aggression." This is necessary, in the sense of not retaliating, if the child is to develop a capacity to use the object. According to Winnicott, when this capacity is impaired in the patient, "in psychoanalytic practice the positive changes that come about in this area can be profound. They do not depend on interpretative work. They depend on the analyst's survival of the attacks, which involves and includes the idea of the absence of a quality change to retaliation. These attacks may be very difficult for the analyst to stand, especially when they . . . [make] the analyst actually do things that are technically bad" (91–92)." Winnicott points out that in these instances we may feel like interpreting, but "this can spoil the process."

Since we understand the narcissistic patient's core problems to be rooted in preverbal existence, or in preverbal senses of the self, we are faced with having to be constantly, ongoingly, for a long time, attending to pathological phenomena while patients have little or no idea what we are doing for them. More than anything else, that is our greatest difficulty. They may sense our helplessness, will have to, in fact, or else will not stay in treatment, but often enough they will not understand treatment, and they may be doing many things in the transference-countertransference arena that are difficult for us to keep quiet about. But we must be made to feel the sense of what has "driven them crazy," those things for which they have no words (the unthought known), not because they are repressed but because they exist within senses of the self that are nonverbal. Arguably, these must be communicated to us nonverbally, through an unconscious dialogue that requires us to "catch our patient's illness," as a supervisee so aptly put it.[9] As we do not wish to catch this illness, or to experience something of the trauma that caused it, or to have to wait out the patient, we may resort to interpretation as a defense to make it go away. Instead, we may have to endure this illness for a long time, with the endurance of a Philippides, at times against acutely intense affective pressure, requiring Herculean strength. Patients will not know what we are giving them, even while they lament the inadequacy of what we are doing for them. Yet the very heart of this work will often need to be enduring, painful disruptions of our sense of core or subjective self, our enduring induced "primitive agonies" and "unthinkable anxieties."

Lulu appeared at my door one day, out of the blue, veneratingly asking my help. She told a moving story of mistreatment by a previous therapist, eventuating in suicide gestures/attempts on her part. After about two years with me, in twice-weekly sessions, she began to place me in internal situations that must have been quite similar to those her previous therapist could not tolerate. I knew both from the patient and from retaliatory letters the previous therapist had written her that the therapist had repeatedly and escalatingly "interpreted" *at* her when the narcissistic countertransference became unbearable. This patient's demanding neediness of the therapist impinged on her in ways that were cumulative and eventually unbearable. In time, these same impingements were obviously becoming manifest in my countertransference. It became exceptionally difficult to endure these inductions without retaliating, even with the help of analytic training and supervision, and the aid of forewarning provided by the previous therapist's torments. Over time the patient's demands for extraanalytic attention reached suicide-threatening form, and her in-session complaints about my treatment of her and about the helplessness of her life caused a great deal of pressure within me. I came to feel quite unresponsive and unsympathetic to her plights, which I felt were overdramatized, whiny, and a function of laziness, a mere unwillingness to exert any effort. This was clearly an effect she had on anyone who got close to her. I came to feel hopeless about assisting her, helpless to change anything. I also began to resent her.

I was unable to be therapeutic until I came to recognize that I was resisting both the full measure of my feelings of helplessness and especially the crippling nature of her disruptions in her sense of core self. She did not have a capacity for object usage, though she presented herself as if she did. But I had had to endure what felt like endless months of misery in order to reach an understanding of her own misery, which she could not begin to convey in words. I had to adopt a sense of her own self-judgments. I felt as ineffectual as she did. I saw her for three more years before her third-party payor disallowed all long-term treatment. In the five years I saw her interpretation played a very small role, if at all a helpful one. What resolved key narcissistic resistances had been the analyst's resolution of complementary counterresistances. Sometimes I told her so, so as to impart some understanding in her of how her symptoms have at times worsened as a result of my own erring, not hers. *But the necessary first step had been my correcting this error, my cognizing my enduring counterresistance, which I had first to have "caught," as it was communicable but not communicative. That is, it had to be caught (like a disease), not told (like an idea).* It was only then that I could adjust myself and respond to her in a more holistic manner, only then I could validate the exigencies of her disturbing inner life, which now found her no longer alone in a miasma. She was able to find a state of meaningful relatedness, of intersubjective and interaffective attunement vis-à-vis dangerously pathogenic material.[10]

SOME COMMON COUNTERTRANSFERENCE RESISTANCES IN THE TREATMENT OF BATTERERS PROPER

On the one hand, we must encounter a negative narcissistic countertransference in our work with batterers.[11] They will inevitably present us with material that speaks clearly of their mistreatment of their loved ones, of those dependent upon them for care and benevolence. Repeatedly, our patients will not recognize these maltreatments as such, or else they will (without realizing) considerably minimize their significance. We will find this phenomenon in even the healthiest of batterer patients. Often we will know of their maltreatments because they are reporting them to us as laments of what they themselves have had to endure. Sometimes it is difficult to grasp that the patient does not recognize the abusiveness of their ways, as exemplified in the adolescent Jacques, who reported with great indignance how a girl who had just fellated him had dared to spit back on him the semen on which she was choking. He reported how he had "of course" had to strike her. Matt told me how he had been forced to strike and choke his young adult son when an argument between them had escalated. It is not uncommon for parents to report that they had needed to slap or knuckle punch their children for their recalcitrance. I suspect that these types of events (to varying degrees of intensity) exist in the lives of some patients of all psychotherapy practices. It is difficult for us to quite hear (i.e., recognize as such) the less severe abuse reports.

However, when we do hear the reports of corporeal or nonphysical abuse, we may struggle with wanting somehow to rescue or champion the afflicted. We may not simultaneously hear our own patient's affliction along with their aberrance. We may "identify with the victim" and defensively deploy an "identification with the aggressor." We must be able to tolerate and "sit with" the pain and helplessness we imagine the abused to have experienced. We must be able to tolerate, know, and contain any outrage we may then feel toward our patient. We must be able to recognize the patient's inability to know and a need to defend against the emotional precipitants and causes of his misdeeds. We will resist these demands upon ourselves, demands that are those of a negative narcissistic countertransference. If we do not accept this narcissistic state in our patients, we are in danger of unwittingly employing an identification with the aggressor. It will be potentiated by our identification with the victim, and we may strike out at–or strike, if you will—the patient with our deployments of quasi interpretations or confrontations, unconsciously serving to punish the patient for their misdeeds transferentially and against their loved ones. Or, we may be punishing the patient for ways they evoke in us mnemic traces of our own traumas. Of course, such errors are exactly how we will ensure that our patients will not develop the capacity to use the object, in the non-exploitative sense that Winnicott meant it. Adjudication or transference needs make for something of a captive audience, susceptible to our own uses of power and control. It behooves us to analyze our own propensities to identify with the aggressor, especially in a climate that I suggest would have us be ashamed of such a defensive strategy. As Racker pointed to the need for us to recognize that even as we are adults and analysts, so too are we children and neurotics, we are also, all of us, a little bit character disordered, narcissistically imperfect, dependent. The analytic superego that would suggest otherwise is a dangerous one.[12]

When Matt reported the incident of fisticuffs with his adult son, I wanted to show him the abusiveness of his behavior and the rationalizations he was employing to avoid this recognition. Instead, I asked a few exploratory questions that made it disappointingly evident he was quite a ways from being able to fathom such ideas. I realized that I had to bide my time, or else risk—for no real potential gain—driving him out of treatment. I had to sit with my feelings and conjure what I understood about why he is thus defended, remember the atrocities with which he grew up, with never anyone to give validation to him for the egregious ways in which he was treated by those who should have loved and cherished him. I had to recall my experience of him as the previously wonderful little boy who would have made a fine adolescent and who would have been a wonderful son to any parent able to open their eyes to the person of him. These were experiences and thoughts I had had of him. I had to mend the split through which I was initially experiencing him when he told me of this incident. I even had to grasp what feelings of inner desperation he had experienced in this incident with this son, feelings of annihilation, of disruption of a sense of his core self, feelings that he had to defend against both during the violent incident and now in its recounting. I had to tolerate ambivalence and whole object relations when it would have been easier in the moment to villainize him, unaware of my action. I had to tolerate the existential anxiety and sadness of living in a world in which we transmit such traumatic themes, from generation to generation, which render lovable people violent and abusive entities—the lovable and the abusive existing in the same self. I also had to tolerate my helplessness to provide absolute and all-reaching, immediate relief for both my patient and his son.[13]

Jacques, cited above in the violent fellatio incident, had no trouble eliciting my inner outrage as he told that story to me. I very much wanted to "nail" him, to strike out at him with my own indignation at his absolute callousness, to belittle him for his inhumanity. I managed not to, but I did flail about a bit, making initial little forays toward that end (which he effectively fended off), until I realized the folly and potential treatment-destructiveness of this countertransference resistance and put it in check. However, that was a rare pitfall for me. More dangerous and commonplace with Jacques was my resistance to noting how truly abusive he was. Early in the analysis he had unsuccessfully tried to alienate me and justify a flight from treatment by horrifying me with reports of his egregious, sadistic interactions with helpless children. By not retaliating and through techniques of psychological reflection, we developed a powerful narcissistic transference-countertransference dialogue in which he idealized me and I identified very strongly with him around aspects of himself that were heroic, in my estimation. Ironically—as I have described him—he felt a righteous anger about various abuses of power in society, abuses of which he had a heightened sense of awareness. At times he was preoccupied with wishes to right particular social injustices; he especially wanted to be able to expose wrongdoers who were being erroneously admired for their dissembled deeds. I especially admired his Titan-like efforts to survive an incredibly abusive father and a shockingly neglectful, betraying, and narcissistically seductive mother. He much more often struck me as a "wonderchild" than as the abusive and sadistic individual he also clearly was. Thus, I had to hold in mind the totality—the hero and the beast—if I was ever going to be able to help him. Yet, even with him, with whom I could more easily err on the side of blindness to his cruelty, I was sorely tempted to villainize when he told me of his striking the young woman.

CHAPTER SEVEN

TRANSFERENCE

> The transference inevitably arises in the analysis.
> —Sigmund Freud (1912)

Freud's (1912) classic "The Dynamics of the Transference" seems to provide an eternally accurate explanation of the source of transference. Of course, the matter is understood today to be even more complex than this, but what a beginning!

Let us bear clearly in mind that every human being has acquired, by the combined operation of inherent disposition and of external influences in childhood, a special individuality in the exercise of his capacity to love—that is, in the conditions which he sets up for loving, in the impulses he gratifies by it, and in the aims he sets out to achieve in it. This forms a *cliché* or stereotype in him, so to speak (or even several), which perpetually repeats itself as life goes on . . . and is indeed itself to some extent modifiable by later impressions. Now our experience has shown that of these feelings which determine the capacity to love only a part has undergone full psychical development; this part is directed towards reality, and can be made use of by the conscious personality, of which it forms part. The other part of these libidinal impulses has been held up in development, withheld from the conscious personality and from reality, and may either expend itself only in phantasy, or may remain completely buried in the unconscious so that the conscious personality is unaware of its existence. Expectant libidinal impulses will inevitably be roused, in anyone whose need for love is not being satisfactorily gratified in reality, by each new person coming upon the scene, and it is more than probable that both parts of the libido, the conscious and the unconscious, will participate in this attitude.

It is therefore entirely normal and comprehensible that the libido-cathexes, expectant and in readiness as they are in those who have not adequate gratification, should be turned also towards the person of the physician. (105–107)

Again, it needs to be recalled that Freud was dealing with object transferences, and that what we are dealing with when the patient batters is a preverbal transference that inheres to a narcissistic relation. That is, when battering, the patient's self and object fields have overlapped (Margolis 1979), and they are in a state in which the object cannot be seen objectively, cannot be seen for what it is. This is the situation in the battering patient, whether or not they are ordinarily able to appreciate the otherness of the object: leading up to, and during, battering they cannot. At that point, there is ego impairment, which may or may not be constant. How much of an observing ego is available to the subject in their interpersonal relations? How much is available for the analyst to ally with? The origins of this transference lie in the preverbal arenas of development. These transferences follow from the senses of self that precede the verbal. The verbal self can only be well-seated when its foundation is a solid bedrock of emergent, core, and subjective senses of self. From this the obvious inference can be drawn that such psychopathology cannot be adequately treated by therapies that address the verbal self to the exclusion of its substrata. Instead, we must broach and breach the "stone wall of narcissism."[1]

Various theoreticians have struggled with this phenomenon over the decades,[2] particularly both Ferecnzi and Aichhorn to begin with, each of whom pioneered early treatment efforts with various types of narcissistic disorders. The term *transference* itself was coined by Waelder (1925) and developed by such theoreticians as Aichhorn, Searles, Little, Spotnitz, Kohut, Wolf, and Margolis. Margolis (1981) tells us that "in the narcissistic transference, the analyst's voice, actions, and words have taken on for the patient the qualities and transcendent importance of his mother when the patient was a baby. And the patient in the narcissistic transference reacts accordingly as though the analyst *were* his mother" (173). Later in the analysis, as the work proceeds and the transference evolves, the analyst is experienced "as like the patient but outside him" (174). Margolis likens these evolving experiences of the analyst to Mahler's autistic and symbiotic stages of development.

Spotnitz conceptualizes that "a two-way emotional transaction is revived and communicated as originating in one locale—the mind of the patient. That transaction, suggestive of a re-experiencing of the ego in the process of formation, is identified as the narcissistic transference" (1985: 186). Margolis again:

> We help the patient develop the negative narcissistic transference in order to mobilize his aggressive feelings and then to study his resistances to expressing these feelings. It is these resistances, stemming from the narcissistic defense, that afford us a glimpse into the origin of the patient's pathology and the dynamics of his conflicts. Our purpose is to ultimately resolve the resistances so that the patient may verbalize the rage repressed in childhood and now displaced onto the analyst. (176)

From a different angle, as Kohut taught us, we might view the narcissistic transference as the patient's need and attempt to procure basic foundational experiences rooted early in life, experiences that were insufficient. Kohut speaks especially of mirroring responses required from the analyst, in which the patient experiences over and over again empathic responses from the analyst at those junctures in which his original pathogenic experiences are activated and ready to be either repeated or else "modified by transference experience," as Freud put it.

How we react to the narcissistic transference will have tremendous and far-reaching consequences. For example, the intersubjectivists have taught us that affective misattunement in the transference-countertransference situation can instantaneously elicit manifestations of whatever diagnosis we are treating. We can then easily succumb to the temptation to blame the patient for his "misbehavior," which in fact we are responsible for having evoked. Object relationists such as Winnicott and Green and the modern psychoanalytic school have taught us that our resistance to the intense displeasure of the negative narcissistic transference may keep us and our patient mired interminably in a status quo resistance.

Jacques so much wanted me not to leave the home after group sessions, but to stay and visit with him as though I were a shift worker rather than a therapist and director. At that time I did not realize that my minor gratifications of this wish, rather than analyzing it, were a resistance on my part to facing the consequences of his rage. Of course he would have felt betrayed by me. While waiting for the group home to open, and knowing that I—his idealized "savior"—was to be its director, he had built up the home as idyllic, the home he had never had. In the months preceding the opening of the home, he was often aware of the coming event and greatly looked forward to it. There must have been signs that I ignored, countertransferentially resisted, as I did not want to face his tremendous transference disappointment. Thus, my unwittingly keeping him stuck in an idealizing transference also prevented progress.

Or, conversely, with many batterers our resistance to narcissistic transference will often drive them from treatment early on. But in the case of Jacques I retarded his progression into an object transference, in which he could be frustrated by me and verbalize and begin to master the frustration. Yet, with many batterers, the temptation to try to foist upon them prematurely a readiness or quasi readiness for object transference is great. Thus we may begin to interpret—even accurately—much too soon, and drive them from treatment.

Terry was court-ordered to treatment. On the one hand, he was interesting and actually had some components of the insight that he believed was his in great abundance. And while he did not have the sensibility to understand the ways in which he grossly failed to do so, it was his sincere wish to provide his children with a nourishing family life. However, his crudeness and pervasive foreclosures of family members' idiomatic self-expressions were very difficult to bear. Instead of the usual group treatment used to fulfill court orders, I was seeing him in couples therapy, with significant effect. He absolutely refused individual therapy, which I perhaps ought to have insisted upon, and I felt under a good deal of pressure to establish some sort of treatment alliance with him before the court-ordered twenty-five hours of treatment had elapsed. These factors bore upon me such that I was greatly tempted at times to confront him in ways that would have insulted him. I do believe that there are many batterers like this, who make the therapist wish to expel back into them the traumatic emotional states they have put into the therapist. These are the cases in which the therapist finds the batterer loathsome or disdainful, nauseating in their other-annihilating or discounting grandiosity.

While, with these patients, there are certainly times when confrontation and interpretation have their places, we must find them when they will be therapeutic. Our temptation will sometimes be to foist the *truth* upon the patient, but these are the retaliatory actions of which Winnicott spoke, in which we fail to withstand the patient's destructiveness at just the time when it is most needed. In chapter 8 I will address additional measures a proactive therapist might take with patients in these maniacal times of narcissistic transference.

In discussing the difficulties of the narcissistic transference and the efficacious handling of it by August Aichhorn, who was his analyst, Kohut remarked (in a reference I cannot locate) something to the effect that "who else but an Aichhorn!" could sit so interminably, humanely, and patiently with an egocentric and self-aggrandizing patient with no idea who the analyst is or what the analyst is doing for him. I was reminded of this struggle when Jessica Lange's character in Jane Smiley's *A Thousand Acres* so poignantly described the great difficulty a child endures when she can never get an offending parent to see his harm to her. In so many ways, especially in those in which the patient's battering-pathognomonic transferences impinge upon the analyst or therapist, the patient has no idea what the therapist must silently sit through, no idea of the often immense countertransference struggles, no idea of what the therapist must contain for him. And, more generally, these more difficult batterer patients often have no other accurate ideas of the therapist either. In any given moment, to the degree that the narcissistic transference is analogous to Mahler's autistic or symbiotic stages, the patient is unable to consider the separateness and the individuation of the analyst, is unable to differentiate between the analyst and himself.

Terry was quite this way. He assumed he knew anything of importance about me. He would cavalierly state assumptions about me that would make me shudder with near nausea. He was not the least bit interested in what I might actually think about anything, and he wanted to expel verbiage and his worldviews in what amounted to nothing more than a monologue, with my purpose being that of a selfobject only.

With these patients, part-object relations predominate, splitting and projective identification fill the stage. Our strong and especially American history of psychoanalytic ego psychology, along with our own counterresistances, would have us want to interpret what is happening to the patient. However, these *clinical infant* phenomena exist because of seriously disrupted domains of experience. These are preverbal domains, core and subjective. *When we cannot enlist a healthy and allied (with us) observing ego with whom we might then be able to articulate what the preverbal experiences are, efforts to interpret or otherwise reach with words are doomed to fail, and fail quickly and decisively. Then our use of words must be like a venue for the carriage of preverbal communication.* Thus it is the nature of the narcissistic transference that the patient can be adequately "spoken to" no more easily than a preverbal child can be reasoned with or mollified by language itself. It is also the nature of narcissistic transference that it demands of analysts and therapists that we honor the patient's need for it. It requires of us that we find ways to identify and address the salient and battering-pathognomonic transference needs in ways that provide preverbal salve, cement, or structure. We do well to remind ourselves, as cited earlier, that "what keeps patients in treatment is their idea [consciously or unconsciously] that *at the same time* they can work maximally toward recreating and resolving past developmental failures or conflicts while minimizing the hurt from affects that attended the earlier maturational failure" (Marshall 1982). The patient must somehow experience us as helpful, potentially helpful, or intriguing. *We must take responsibility for this occurring.*

Considering that narcissistic transferences have their roots in preverbal domains of experience, we ought also take note that they revolve around initially *unobservable (i.e., unobservable by the patient's ego)* threats *to the self's continuity of being*, around basic and biological integrity and security experiences, around senses of being loved and lovable, around senses of being able to find contact with, comfort and solace from, or admiration from a loved other. Our narcissistic patient will not know when these senses of self are threatened and *instead of knowing* and struggling with such experiences will automatically *act* so as to alter the threatening situation, as it is experienced. Our patient's relevant narcissistic issues will inevitably arise in the analysis. If we wish him to ever develop serviceable insight into such things as his tendencies to impulsivity, identification with the aggressor, splitting, projection, impaired empathy, etc., we will have to allow ourselves to experience and address narcissistic transferences through an understanding of resistances that are rooted in preverbal domains of experience.

SOME CLINICAL EXAMPLES

Terry and Alice, who felt misconstrued as criminals when they considered themselves rather to be "unable to handle our feelings sometimes" (as Alice stated it), provide further instruction. Both of them came from what appeared to be chronically neglectful families with the psychological sensibilities of a lower species. Indeed, I had a strong pseudospeciating tendency with Terry. Both described impoverished childhoods they nonetheless did not recognize as such. Terry was an auto mechanic, Alice a waitress in usually working-class restaurants. They had a rather "cute" (is the best way I can find to say it) coupleness about them, and they worked hard to pay the bills, set a little something aside, and raise their children well.

Terry so often spoke with such pervasive derision of his wife and of their marriage, and presented himself as so Neanderthalic that, as I have acknowledged, it was often difficult not to behave beratingly toward him.[3]

Instead, I looked for inroads with this man whose wife was sincere about and intent upon staying with him. I especially sought to grasp both intellectually and affectively why he acted this way, so that I would be able to make him feel understood in such a fashion that he might proceed toward an increased sense of core and subjective selves and an increased observing ego. He was extremely devaluing and denigrating of all psychotherapies and acted as though the only way that I could be helpful would be by grasping the wisdom of his narcissistic world, family, and marital views. I bided my time, making small contacts with him where I could, until he began playfully to be able to experience my little jestings and *joining* or *maturational interpretations.* For example, when he was presenting a sorry old refrain about his wife's infidelity and the impossibility of his ever being able to trust her again, I made what was an obvious interpretation about his repeating a traumatic theme of his childhood, an area that we had just been discussing. I presented myself in a way that allowed me to make simultaneous contact with his longing self, his stubborn self, and the part of him that wants to be admired by me but could not begin to say so. We were able to laugh together at this juncture, at this moment in treatment.

But I was only able to reach him because I had sat with his narcissistic transference for some time, and would no doubt have had to continue doing so. (Financial constraints for this working-class family finally made it truly impossible for them to stay in treatment—a situation therapists are faced with all too often if they choose to try to accept into longer-term treatment those cases that originated through court order.) I had to honor his need to espouse his views, even though they were views of an other-obliterating and terribly egocentric nature. He still needed to be heard, even if I found his views thoroughly distasteful. I also had to tolerate his manner of speaking, which was often quite pressured and difficult to listen to. He would sit on the edge of his seat, and speak with a kind of unself-conscious urgency that allowed no one else to be heard—indeed, that allowed no one else to even begin to speak. I often wanted to be able to silence him, so that I would not feel the invasion, the induction of his chaos-feeling anxiety, of the inner "screeching" of my self when he prattled on. It left no space in which I could feel that I might exist as a person in relation to him. Eventually, in a long-term treatment, not available here, this conveyance of a negative transformational object could have been usefully interpreted to him, though against formidable resistance on his part.

Jacques originally arrived at treatment, he later told me, thinking of the fun he'd have dispatching this latest in a series of psychotherapists, inpatient and outpatient alike, whom he'd been exposed to over the years of his family's involvement with Child Protection Services. Indeed, when he began work with me, he was a brash and highly self-aggrandizing young man—the picture of a classic juvenile delinquent who needs no one. He spoke brazenly about his cruel exploits and about the absolute folly of the "establishment," which had professed a wish to help him and whose principal players he saw as weak, ineffectual, and highly hypocritical. He imagined himself a world-class mountaineer—fantasizing himself a great war chief who undertakes vision quests atop Montana's most inaccessible mountains, able to vanquish any foe for the sake of his oppressed people. He also fancied himself a kind of godsend to women. Curiously, he liked to think of himself as a tormentor of any sniveling weaklings who dared to present their vulnerability to him, such individuals seeming to represent his vulnerable child self that had been unable to protect him. As I understood all these presentations to be necessary props against a lifetime of chronic neglect and severe abuse, I did not confront or interpret anything for a very long time. Instead, I set myself the task of honoring his need for no insight, honoring his incapacity for empathy for his victims, and honoring his self-aggrandizement. In short, I honored his narcissistic transference; at that point he could not look upon me as an expert at all.

Matt, whose narcissistic transference needs I was not originally honoring, let me know about it through his acting-out. I assumed more capacity for self-observation than he possessed. When he jumped up and brandished his fist, I kept my composure, told him it would be best for him to be seated, and when he did not immediately comply, I eased away from him and called the police. The phone call snapped him back to a bit more of a thinking posture, he backed off, and I suggested he leave at that point in order to avoid arrest, that we would talk again in short order. He did leave right away and, in fact, passed the police on his way out the building. Fortunately, the police arrived literally two minutes after I called; however, no longer in physical danger, I did not give them my patient's name, so as to protect the treatment and his confidentiality.

I telephoned this patient not long after he'd left my office and scheduled a session that immediately ushered in a new phase of treatment. As I have said with different emphasis elsewhere, I was able to connect with him through words that spoke of his experience of acutely disrupted narcissistic equilibrium, of the exigency of the disruption of his sense of core self. He felt deeply understood, and deeply moved by my nonpunitive and treatment-motivated posture with him. His narcissistic transference has predominated, but one that I am sitting with, only seeking object transference articulations where prudent. I have not been pushed by my wish for him to see more than he could at any given point, *but have instead followed him as the guide for the pace and type of interventions I have made.* Or, better put still, I have tried to follow the path of determining what kinds of interventions he was able to utilize at any given point. Very often, this requires that the therapist sees certain kinds of destructiveness in the patient's life that the patient cannot, and efforts to point them out would be countertherapeutic.

Pablo originally came to treatment at the behest of his wife. Initially disdainful toward and distrustful of all psychotherapies, he presented himself as a "tough guy" who also just happened to be highly intelligent and educated. His tough guy persona was in ascendance over any identity as a thinker, although he espoused contemplative values. He was proud to nickname himself "Kid," which he said was "dick" spelled backward. He spoke ambivalently about barroom brawls he'd engaged in, in which he had either been hurt or had rather badly hurt others. His history was replete with homicidal-intensity and homicidal-quality affects and parental relationships. For example, at very young ages, he and his brother were taught to kickbox each other, with official kickboxing rules, as their father's way of helping them with conflict resolution. This same brother was killed as a young man when he got caught up in a barroom fight of his own. My patient's parents psychically enshrined this deceased brother, in whose shadow Pablo felt he had to live whenever he sought out parental attentiveness.

In weekly sessions for about ten years, Pablo slowly began to be interested in a relationship with me in which he could feel recognized and appreciated for the gifted and talented man he is. He is very bright, psychologically minded, and enjoyed bantering about various psychoanalytic and systemic notions. He is an artist of considerable renown who could not incorporate into his sense of himself the beauty of his accomplishments or the keenness of his intellect. The early years of his work with me, while punctuated by quasi interpretations, were marked therapeutically by an attention to his hunger for a mirroring transference (Kohut 1984), in which he could test out and incorporate numerous aspects of his identity as well as build up preverbal psychic structure.

After some years, then, of a positive narcissistic transference, he moved resoundingly into a negative one in which he tormented me, for about a year, belittling psychoanalysis and me and repeatedly threatening me with precipitous termination of treatment. This period moved into a quiescent state in which he seemed self-reflective and appreciative of my not having abandoned him during the time he expressed derision and hatred of me. Some months went along in this state when he suddenly announced that he was taking a six-week hiatus from treatment and would "just look upon it as an experiment," and cavalierly—he was quite cognizant of this attitude—decide whether he ought to resume after that break or not.

It was evident to me in these communications that he was furious with me and that his unconscious intent was to make me feel as disempowered as he had felt growing up and as he continues to feel in critical aspects of his life. However, he seemed to have no idea that I might be relieved to be rid of his negative narcissistic transference and of his intense and homicidal-feeling transference rage at me. He could only imagine that my reaction to this news would be one of disappointment at the loss of a prized analysand; it did not occur to him that I might have any number of patients who are pleasanter to work with than he. How much I may have been counterresisting the rage inherent in this case is an open question, and one that I may never be able to answer. He did leave treatment and in two years now has not returned.

Clearly, he needed to be able to verbalize his affects rather than act them out through leaving. I can see in retrospect that I may have "overjoined" him, did not recognize when he had developed the ability to receive certain interpretations and confrontations about his inner life. Was I also avoiding his rage? Was it inevitable that he would have to enact a leaving of the other in his treatment? Had I foreseen this or understood better his need to be isolated, to wallow in being misunderstood, would it have mattered? Certainly, I had established a forum with him in which there were many opportunities to interpret. He had quite wed himself to *le negatif*,[4] and may have found his primary psychic gratifications in some sort of repudiation of interpersonal life. Given his intelligence and his psychological awareness, might I have engaged him in an object-transferential wondering had I begun interpreting and interpretively exploring this realm a few years before his leaving? Now, to have done so, however, does bring me back to the question of my possible avoidance of transference aggression. He was superficially pleasant and appreciative and saw me as some kind of guru for quite some time. Yet I knew of his disdain for so many. Was there sufficent observing ego for the analyst to engage? Could I have managed to establish a more classical treatment alliance after he had been in an ego-enhancing transference for so long? Could he have made this transition had I been able to hear his capacity for it?

Another patient, while not to my knowledge a batterer, does allow another helpful angle on the narcissistic transference. Franklin was self-referred for relationship difficulties, being unable to sustain either friendships or a romantic relationship. He presented many difficulties with procrastination and incompletion of work as well. He was challenging, suspicious of my ability to help, flippant, and critical at numerous points in any given session—all from the beginning of treatment. Early on he expressed wholly unrealistic expectations for "quick cures" (even being highly educated and intelligent and knowing full well the long-term nature of psychoanalytic treatment). He quickly established a habit whereby he became intensely angry and gesticulated with disgust at the end of sessions: how useless the session had been and how incredible that the session was completed, with my once more having given him nothing useful! While he was desirous of interpretations, which I gave him and for which he even expressed periodic appreciation—even admiration—I was well aware that the bulk of our work had nothing to do with language as such, that the work was happening preverbally, in the building up of the narcissistic transference-countertransference situation/relationship.

He was criticizing me mightily and quite effectively putting me into a high level of anxiety as sessions approached; conversely and simultaneously, I found a pleasant anticipation about his imminent arrival, as I felt something of a connection to him as to an admirably recalcitrant, doggedly rebellious, determined-to-survive son. I would sometimes imagine him suddenly jumping up off the couch, yelling threateningly and admonishingly, "What the hell are you doing there anyway?" I understood that it was necessary for him to communicate these feelings to me preverbally, as he had no direct access to communicating in words and affect what he grew up with and what he had subsequently endured. His childhood was dominated by a tyrannical, chronically screaming and belittling mother, and a mostly absentee father, who was impassive and who took every opportunity to escape a wife he could not stand up to. Thus, I knew that I had to repeatedly tolerate, detoxify, and thereby make available for reintrojection those inductions that he had to put into me, inasmuch as he could not tell me about them. Again, I had to be respectful of the narcissistic transference. It was necessary that I see what was in him by his expelling it. It had to exist as a part of my experience. After about two years of weekly sessions, he began to exhibit some awareness of and curiousity about how I was experiencing him, how he was affecting me. He began to associate freely to musings about how his critical and negative nature must have something to do with his relationship difficulties. He is beginning to consciously experience some appreciation of his therapist.

However, I now believe that such a shift often ushers in its own unique pitfalls, a considerable treatment-destructive potential. A capacity to register the therapist as someone actually valued may bring a threat of the loss of the negative, *le negatif*. Franklin used to hide in the basement as a child, ostensibly seeking solace from a destructive mother. However, at this time he was also beginning to develop a misfit identity; more to the point, he was beginning to invest himself in this identity. We have to at least hypothesize that whatever maternal care his mother might have had to offer was being rejected. He became something subhuman, "the thing that lives in the basement." He has perpetuated this identity. It is his psychic path of least resistance to gratification, to having anything to be invested in. To come to value the analyst at this juncture becomes dangerous, as that valuing begins to threaten the maintenance of the no-object, that absence which is his passion.[5] Masturbation, marijuana, eating for fullness when doing so worsens a medical condition—all these are his autoerotic gratifications, complemented by the attachment to the no-thing and the impassioned laments about his misfit station in life. There is no risk, no trouble to meet the real other—alloeroticism is unnecessary. If he comes to value the analyst too much, it seems to me that this dilemma must be verbalized or in some fashion contained, or else he will have to enact it, will have to make the analyst one of the no-things, will have to leave the analyst, which is probably just what Pablo had to do.[6]

I have tried in this chapter to give a living flavor of the manifestations of the narcissistic transference and the analyst's observation and experience of this transference with which we must grapple so directly in our treatment of what drives battering. It is the treatment of these underlying psychic entities, without which battering could not occur, that we must address. It is the transformation of these initially nonverbalizable states that must attend the remission of battering.

CHAPTER EIGHT
JOINING TECHNIQUES

As stated earlier, Jacques was originally referred to me for treatment of his budding juvenile delinquency, his bullying of children smaller than himself, and for the purpose of helping him recover psychologically from a nearly life-ending incident at the hands of his stepfather. By way of a reminder, at fourteen he was already a therapy-savvy boy, having already proudly "defeated" an indeterminate number of therapists, both outpatient and inpatient, in his young life. Years later, he often referred to our early days together and how "cocky" and confident he felt upon referral that here was yet another therapist to be pleasantly vanquished. Early on he was self-indulgently reporting to me some of his bullying escapades. I especially recall one such incident in which he reported having taunted a young girl on the school bus, until she was brought to tears. Resisting my urge to yield to my identification with this unfortunate little girl, and "confront" my patient under the guise of therapeutic intervention, I took quite a different approach. I began to express considerable interest in all the sadistic minutiae: how he was able to skillfully escape detection and admonishment for his misdeeds, specifically how he taunted her, what things he said, how intensely he pointedly and purposely projected his intimidating methods, how refined his methods were, how quickly he'd brought her to tears, etc. I quite cognizantly let him see that not only was I able to be *as* sadistic as he, but in fact I queried him as to why he had not employed more egregious methods than he had. In little time at all he was objecting to my suggestions, telling me that there was no way that HE was going to do THAT, that he knew what it was like to be treated that way, that his stepfather had done way too much of that sort of thing to him, and he'd be damned if he was now going to do that with this girl, who was as defenseless as he was against his stepfather. What is the theory of technique behind such interventions on my part? Why did I not merely point out to him that he was reenacting his relationship with his stepfather, with himself now in the role of aggressor?

Let me introduce these concepts with Hyman Spotnitz, the father of Modern Psychoanalysis:

> Preoedipal resistance patterns are rarely responsive to objective understanding. The term "joining techniques" is loosely applied to a number of basically similar interventions to manage these patterns, particularly those reflecting preverbal functioning. In making the interventions, the therapist supports and may even reinforce continued operation of the resistance until the patient "develops the awareness and ego strength to replace it with a more adaptive and controlled behavior pattern (Marshall 1982:87)." (Spotnitz 1985:263)

Spotnitz provides thorough coverage of modern psychoanalytic techniques, among which joining occupies a central position.

Joining techniques, then, are those (noninterpretive) techniques we employ with narcissistic, preoedipal, or selfobject resistances. That is, they are the techniques we rely upon when the patient would be wounded by, or otherwise unable to utilize, interpretations or any other cognitively based interventions *that require the patient to call upon observing ego in order to process the intervention.* We ought to simultaneously think of these methods as those we utilize *when the patient's preoedipal, preverbal, or narcissistic psychostructural underpinnings are in need of strengthening,* or when they are poorly formed or overtaxed by the effort of repression of too much aggression, frustration, and disappointment.

It is the preoedipal patient's inability to observe certain disconcerting aspects of their inner life that necessitates joining. In this vein, then, I will at times be saying "preoedipal patient" to refer to any patient who is either regularly or momentarily (i.e., at that particular moment) diminished by a preoedipal resistance. The same qualification applies to my use of the terms *narcissistic* or *preverbal* patients.

It is also of great importance to understand that joining techniques are powerful tools in the development of the narcissistic transference, wherein the narcissistic or preoedipal resistances must ultimately be resolved. Insight alone about preverbal pathogenic traumata is useless, *if the attendant unrememberable experiences are not activated in the treatment relationship, where they can then be dealt with more than intellectually or abstractly.* The patient's resistances to consciously reexperiencing/remembering these traumata, which actually punctuate or predominate his unconscious and defensive life, must be lived and overcome inside the transference.

Margolis tells us:

The preoedipal patient arrested at the narcissistic phase says No to the world. He defends his fragile emotional economy by turning a deaf ear not only to the stimuli that press upon him from without, but also to his own psychic processes. In these circumstances, any attempt to address his problems with rational interpretations and insights meets a stone wall, at best of incomprehension, at worst of negation. . . . How to deal with such an unyielding resistance pattern? (1994 [1983]:222–223)

From much work with schizophrenic and other narcissistic patients, Spotnitz (1985, 1987) gradually evolved the notion that the way to exert an influence for change on these patients was for the therapist to ally himself with the patient's position against change. This required that the therapist align himself in favor of the resistance. He was to forego all efforts at inducing the patient to give up his defensive pattern. (222–223).

It is only when narcissistic resistances are resolved that more traditional treatment methods are brought into play. Margolis (1979, 1994 [1983]) gives us a good feel for the diversity and wide application of joining techniques. He particularly addresses (1979, 1981) the ways in which joining and other modern psychoanalytic techniques can be used to evolve the crucial and indispensable narcissistic transference.

Marshall succinctly states:

Resistances, when based on defenses evolved well after the preverbal era, can be met successfully with clarifications, confrontations, and interpretations. When resistances to treatment clearly reflect functioning stemming from a preverbal era, I believe that the classical psychoanalytic interventions have little utility, and, in some instances, can be damaging, especially to children, adolescents, and those with weak or immature egos. Joining techniques oriented toward supporting *and* resolving narcissistic resistances are the approaches of choice. (1982:62)

Marshall goes on to give complexly thought out case examples of an assortment of modern psychoanalytic interventions that provide a sense of their potency and broad applicability.[1]

As a number of modern psychoanalytic writers caution, I wish to under-score here that these techniques ought not to be used as gimmicks, without thorough supervision, or without grounding in a broader psychoanalytic context of treatment. Additionally, before deploying some of these inter-ventions we ought to have a fair predictive sense of what they will yield, and we ought to be quite certain of the transference and countertransference antecedents and consequents relevant to any such deployment.[2]

JOINING TECHNIQUES WITH BATTERERS

To my way of experiencing it, there is one big difference between court-or-dered and self-referred batterer patients. When those who are adjudicated enter treatment, they tend to be more guarded, angry, or at times (and treatment-obstructively) quasi-acquiescent or reactively acquiescent than are self-referred patients. They have been criminalized and often may have felt humiliated by police, prosecutors, and the court, as well as by victims' advocates. They have been branded "batterer" or "wife-beater," whereas the self-referred patient is usually not even identified as being prone to using violence and does not feel in need of absolution, face-saving, or re-lease from the justice or "correctional" system.

Terry, to whom I referred, along with his wife Alice, in chapters 1 and 7 in no way conceptualizes himself to be a batterer or to have problems with im-pulse control or sensitivity to others. He appeared for some time to be whol-ly unable to consider his wife's laments, as stated in couples therapy. His very reactions to her complaints often demonstrated the accuracy of same: that he does not listen to her point of view, that he is "always right" (he made no pretense of trying to consider her views). He would usually chuckle at her communications, further infantilizing, frustrating, and deriding her. This scenario occurred so often that I more than once was unable to act with fore-thought as opposed to rationalization of my actions, and then I "confront-ed" him with his behavior. He would then tend to dismiss me as being just another arm of the law who could not understand his plight. Only when I would focus on the specifics of his own rationalizations, and respond un-derstandingly and supportively to his perceived plight did I make contact with him.[3] These interventions were executed so that there would be no room to assume that I was equating their rationalizations with rational thought. For a number of sessions the same old refrains issued from him, without any indication that my approach would bear fruit. After about fifteen sessions he began to soften considerably in his position, at times offering brief acknowledgments of his awareness of his recalcitrance toward and absolute blaming of his wife. At these instances, which have occurred three times in ten sessions now (there have been a total of twenty-five sessions), he has even been open to exploration of the whys of his behavior, citing childhood events and patterns as well as his present fears of vulnerability with his wife, indicating that he finds his blaming positions self-protective. He worries that she will leave him outright, or repeat her single experience of infidelity. However, any sustaining of communicating this vulnerability openly and without retaliation or defensiveness is still fleeting.

Many adjudicated batterers will either say that their wives deserved the violence they perpetrated or else that maybe it would have been better if they hadn't been violent but anyone in their situation would have been. Often these statements are so objectively ludicrous and negating of the spouse that it is difficult to keep one's mouth shut, to not chastise the patient. However, our self-restraint pays in dividends when instead we are able to supportively and uncensoriously help the patient try to communicate to us what transpires leading up to and during battering. When he knows that we understand his situation, and are still accepting of him, he is able to continue to communicate, searchingly. So, as a brief example:

P: Anyone would've hit her if she'd done that to them!
A: She must've seemed pretty intense!
P: She WAS pretty intense, I'll tell ya.
A: It must be very difficult when that sort of thing is happening.
P: Yes.

Extremely simple. Yet we can be blinded to the obvious when hearing their stories. But if we do so listen, we can then easily proceed to an exploration of the batterer's inner experience leading up to battering. At these junctures the experience-near concepts of narcissistic disequilibrium, disruptions of the sense of core self, and Winnicott's unthinkable/psychotic anxieties are helpful ones for us to hold in mind, as we attempt to build a language with each patient that will give voice to the intolerable feelings they are defending against with their intimidation and battering.

Matt serves as a good example of how we might use these theoretical constructs to treatment advantage. Mentioned in chapter 7, Matt is the patient whose physical threat necessitated my phoning the police. Upon exploring this session with him when we next met, which was in fact the very next day by mutual decision, Winnicott's *going to pieces*, which I have amended to *flying to pieces* or *exploding to pieces* for batterers, was especially useful. Our exploration of what had occurred within him just before he physically threatened me, our shared efforts to find language to reflect his experience adequately (see Bollas's [1987] *transformational object*, when language becomes the tool or venue of transformation), these efforts were invaluably facilitated by my knowledge of his *unthinkable anxieties*. Matt was actually exuberant to find me able to verbally grasp, with utter acceptance, an experience he had struggled with for most of his life, an experience with which he hitherto felt totally isolated, having encountered no one in his life who understood it. Indubitably, the manner of my handling of his threats the previous evening, my telephoning him to check on his condition once he'd arrived at his home, and my sheer willingness, not to mention my wish, to still treat him when he'd expected to be rejected and ousted from treatment all contributed to his relief and experience of union and security with me. A positive narcissistic transference was opened.[4] For a couple of years he would refer to this event with appreciation and awe, as it continued to serve for a representation to him of the security he has found in our relationship in contradistinction to the abject neglect, abuse, and abandonment he grew up with.

To have accomplished this with him, it was necessary that I allow him the opportunity to attribute responsibility solely to me for his threatening me. Though he did in fact accept a great deal of responsibility himself, this was clearly aided by communications from me at our beginning to process the prior evening's events:

A: What did I do that was so inflaming last night?

P: I truly don't know. One minute I was calm, and the next I was on my feet, standing over you with my fist cocked. I don't think you did anything.

A: I obviously really missed something very important last night. I mean, it's my job to notice how events in the session are affecting you.

P: No, I just have this bad temper. I've always had it. It's not your fault.

A: Perhaps your always having had it isn't my fault. But why didn't I see that you were upset?

P: Well, it woulda been nice if you'd've noticed I was getting pissed off. I DID try to tell you.

A: I really missed it.

It was this effort on my part to instantially attenuate the pressure of his narcissistic defense by offering myself as a correct target for the constructive verbal communication of his frustration with, disappointment in, and aggression toward me, in a reversal of his self-blaming, that relieved enough pressure and freed enough observing ego that we were able to explore his unthinkable anxieties, i.e., that made them thinkable. It was clear to him that I was not (countertransferentially) insisting that he (transferentially) live anew the blamings he was so accustomed to in his formative years, in which any efforts on his part to attend to his personal, psychological rights would be met by his various caregivers as unacceptable infringements upon their own narcissistic equilibrium. As one example of a myriad, should he have protested the extreme intersibling favoritism that he was victimized by, he would have been yet further denigrated.

Another case: Jacques. Reviewed earlier, I will revisit this intervention now, with additional considerations. About three years and approximately four hundred hours into his analysis, at the point of the intervention, he was in a community residential treatment center, of which I was program director and where I was continuing to treat him. (He had been unable to be contained in shelter care and in a number of foster homes, including therapeutic foster homes. Jacques and I had, by this time, already established a very powerful positive narcissistic transference, with both idealizing and twinship features (Kohut 1984). Thus, *I had tremendous psychological leverage with him, an absolute necessity in interventions like the following.*[6]

Jacques had been given a directive by a youth care worker, a directive that brought immediate and vehement invective and objection from him. In fact, the directive referred to the cessation of a sexually provocative interaction he was indulging in, this particular injunction, then, being highly poignant for him, who had developed a strong defense against a sexually provocative, sexually overstimualting mother by means of himself becoming, in his words, "a player." This defense existed against his extremely potent, disavowed experiences of his mother's narcissistic and libidinal violations. So to have to endure this particular injunction by a youth care worker, especially in front of the teenage girl he was "playing"—he was rather blatantly and coarsely attempting to seduce her, right on the street—was powerfully disruptive for him. He came storming into the house with a rage unprecedented in my direct experience of him. He was intimidating in an intensity that reflected the pervasive and near-actualized homicidal phenomenology of the first fourteen years of his life. It really felt as though the entire house would just explode under the impact of his emotionally violent and imminently, physically violent outburst.

I was the only person in the house at that time who had nearly enough training to attempt to manage this situation without resorting to calling the police (which in this case would have meant his arrest and the jeopardizing of his placement in the center) or using other strong-arm methods like "takedowns," which the staff were trained to do. However, I even doubted quite seriously that such a physical intervention method would have been effective, as his rage was so enormous, he was so "pumped" with adrenaline, and he was a young man of considerable physical strength. The potency of his outburst, too, which can hardly be conveyed verbally with sufficient precision, was such that he had already shocked into inefficacy all the staff (not to mention fellow residents) in the house.

So, I decided to jump into the fray. I attempted to merely immediately deescalate him with verbal commands from me, to whom his strong narcissistic transference relationship, I reasoned, might suffice to psychically "grab hold of him" and bring him back from the brink. The futility of that hope was immediately apparent, and, as we were in an exigent crisis, I decided to "mirror" his emotional state, in the hope that I might thereby be able to instantiate myself (as a good internal object) into the subjective space in which he was currently residing. I therefore matched his outward and emotional intensity, step for step. Verbally, I was merely telling him what was behaviorally expected of him at this point, but emotionally I was meeting him in his over-the-top "exploding into pieces" rage. He yelled; I yelled. He yelled more loudly; I yelled more loudly. This exchange went on probably about five to ten times. (It was about three years from the event to my first writing about it, though the actual number of such exchanges may have even eluded me immediately following the incident.)

He began to threaten to run away, gathered some things, and started on his way out the door.[6] I knew that if I physically grabbed him he might erupt into intense violence. However, trusting my own strength coupled with his concern for me, and by now having a highly trusted staff member nearby (and being mentally prepared to suddenly go sprawling across the floor with him), I threw both my arms around his waist as he started for the door.[7] I do not remember my words, but my message to him must have resonated clearly within him, that I was willing to enter his hell in order to save him from it. Instead of erupting into violence, his body went completely slack; I set him down on a nearby couch. And he began to sob. He was suddenly most sincerely apologetic and remorseful about what he then interpreted as himself acting exactly like the abusive stepfather who had almost killed him. He wailed, "How could I do that to you, man?!"

He was also impressed by my having been able to self-consciously enter his intensely aggressive output arena, if I may call it that, in such a way that I was not out of control myself. He quite marveled at that. "God! HOW did you do that? I mean, you were angry, I could see that, but I mean you were in control of yourself! I could see that you knew what you were doing. *I* didn't; I had no control over my anger. I need to learn how to DO that!"

This event seemed to usher in, or perhaps even sponsor, an incipient depressive stage for him, reminiscent of the passage from Melanie Klein's *paranoid-schizoid* position to the *depressive position*.[8] He spent a fair amount of time in ensuing months recalling, with at times a near paralyzing grief reaction, some of the atrocities he had endured over the years. So strong was his pain that I remember being called into the group home one night, his having asked the staff to call me, the staff doing so with palpable foreboding. But I was still unprepared for what greeted me upon my entry into the room where he sat. The lights were very dim, and the pain, the grief in the room was so powerful that I felt a strong wish to bolt from there. When we spoke to each other, Jacques's pain was of such poignant intensity and quality that words cannot begin to do justice to the experience. He sobbed and sobbed and asked pitifully why his life had had to be the way it was. My heart bled for him, and we sobbed together.

In my multiple roles as director, I once had occasion to take him on an errand that allowed us time to detour for a pleasant drive to a prominent overlook of our beautiful valley and its surrounding sublime mountains. It was just before Christmas, very cold—maybe about zero degree Fahrenheit—at about four in the afternoon. There was a heavy snowpack, new snow, and an indescribable evening alpenglow that is unimaginable, I should think, to anyone who has never been there. We climbed to a high spot, shivering in the wind, transported by nature—in a mutual aesthetic moment, and he began to speak of the childhood he had always secretly longed for. It was most compelling and poignant. He imagined being loved and admired, with parents who had some equanimity. On our drive home, in heavy dusk, he gazed into warmly Christmas-lit homes and spoke further of his imagined childhood. He related a scene in which his father would be reading a book in the living room, in front of the window, drinking coffee; he and his sister would be nearby, essentially basking in the ambience, his mother visible and audible in the kitchen, happily preparing a holiday meal.

Time passed, and after a long idealizing transference Jacques began to voice his various disappointments in me, especially revolving around my not having somehow *become* his father. He used to long for me to take him in as a foster child. He felt quite hurt by and angry about his having to pay for sessions, after having had the state pay my fee until he was eighteen. He had moved at eighteen to a nearby Northwest state, to live with the ex-wife of his biological father and his half-sister, neither of whom he had seen since he was two years old. The stepmother held out the promise of taking care of him, which included payment of his continued work with me over the phone. But then she, too, let him down, deciding after he moved there that, first, she could not pay for his psychotherapy and, later, that she and her daughter could no longer manage to live with him. At this writing Jacques is twenty-one years old, and he has continued to check in with me about once every six months for the last several years. While he clearly needs further treatment, it is also clear that he maintains an internalized good object (paternal and maternal) through his past work with and periodic revisitings of me. His anger at me for being only his analyst is in need of analytic working through. His senses of core self and intersubjective self are in need of solidification. Further inner capacity for affect regulation and narcissistic equilibrium needs to develop. The stability of reliable inner objects is not what we would want it to be.

But he has not lived out the life that he was blueprinted for. It was clear to me and to those supervisors and peers familiar with his case that he was at risk of developing a homicidal route in his young life. His fantasies of shooting fellow high school students whom he felt were abusive to him, tormenting him with racial epithets and less overt prejudice—these could easily have been enacted many times over.

However, what a pity that society merely jettisoned him and any responsibility to him when he reached the magical age of eighteen! He was left with nowhere to live, once his stepmother kicked him out, and with absolutely no means of paying for a continuing psychoanalytic psychotherapy that had arguably saved his life and the lives of anyone he might have otherwise murdered.

MATT

If he is to truly alter his deleterious life path, Matt will need to attain the same kinds of psychostructural goals that Jacques was denied. He continues to depend on a variety of self-soothing strategies that all but foreclose any opportunity for him to come to know himself deeply or to recognize and have the psychic strength to alter the multitude of interrelated compulsive repetitions. Like so many batterer cases, this is another where financial and psychical inhibitors coincide. Impulsivity and the need to be taken care of by a powerful father figure allowed him to badly misjudge a financial investment opportunity, putting up much more money than he could afford to lose. He was conned and lost tens of thousands, along with any ongoing income. Among other financial hardships, he is now faced with being able to afford only monthly contacts with me, the only patient I have maintained at such a low frequency, in the hope that he will find his way back to regular sessions, hopefully a minimun of twice weekly.[9]

After a long period of believing that he was doing well, inasmuch as he had had no temper outbursts for a couple of years—a completely unprecedented event—he has nonetheless, even at this low frequency of contact, come to be a much better student and observer of himself, and a much better reporter of his inner life. He now recognizes something of his addictive relationship to a variety of objects and activities (which I am purposely not going into, owing to the smallness of the town in which we live). However, I do not imagine that it will be possible for him to work out his narcissistic or object resistances within the transference as long as we cannot meet more often. Yet, rather impressively, he has clearly continued to progress analytically in spite of this.

Looking back on past notes, I am struck by a worry that his resistance to a negative narcissistic transference might have reached treatment-destructive proportions. I saw that he was at a risky time in his analysis, that he might flee. Has his reduction in frequency been the resistance that it usually is when patients cite it, rather than an unequivocal financial reality as I have accepted it? Is this how he has managed to keep his rage outside of the transference? Is he afraid that his anger will poison his good feelings about and good representations of me?[10]

MANNY: A RETROSPECTIVE LOOK AT PSYCHOPATHY

Manny was self-referred for domestic violence. He feared that if he did not enter treatment his wife would leave him. After several months his marital relationship was back on what he considered to be stable ground, and I was not able to keep him in treatment. I did, however, predict what later occurred. A year after his precipitous termination, he asked to return to psychotherapy, saying that his wife had left him, he was distraught. He was rather solicitous regarding his not having "listened to" me a year earlier. He lamented that had he stayed in treatment he might not have driven his wife away.

The following paragraph was written when Manny was still in treatment on this second round. He stayed for perhaps two years before again leaving precipitously. After this second departure, I recognized the central and life-determining psychopathy in him that I had theretofore ignored. In fact, his case is one that has helped me recognize psychopathy, which is often well disguised. I will present the next paragraph as it was originally written, when I was unaware of what I am now calling his psychopathic substrate. I will afterward discuss the psychopathic features of the case. (As the following paragraph is displaced in time, I will italicize the entire passage, so that it stands clearly apart.)

He has now been back in treatment for another year, and has been talking rather progressively much of the time. He is clearly in a positive narcissistic transference, and is growing more stable as a result. He is no longer underemployed and is developing more empathy for the two children he left behind across the country three years ago when he eloped with an exciting young woman, the children's nanny, with whom he felt a kind of symbiotic bliss that was not destined to last. His relative lack of empathy for his children used to induce wishes in me to "confront" him, to "show" him what he was doing to them. Instead, I recognized pertinent causal factors like his experience of his father as one of a threat of being engulfed; and I noted that his descriptions of his mother are practically nonexistent, or that what descriptions exist still leave her nondescript, a nonentity. It will have to be confirmed or ruled out in the transference that she was vacant for him early in life, or else possibly, though I doubt it, that he has repressed more sentient images of her because of threatening concomitants. Again, it will have to be manifest in and resolved in the transference, which is a shorthand way of saying that it must be manifest in and resolved in the transference-countertransference relationship.

Well, Manny announced one day that the business he worked for had been sold and that there would be no place for him with the new owners. He therefore was moving to another part of Montana, which would allow him to better pursue his impassioned wilderness avocation, the original reason for his coming to the state. He indicated that he would be ceasing treatment, was not interested in continuing via phone contacts, and he left with no semblance of attachment to me. It was with this same insouciance that he had left the first time around as well. The sense I registered of this, i.e., my countertransference reaction to it, was one of having been hit by a ton of bricks unawares. I was as insignificant to him as could be! And I was taken by surprise by this.

How to distinguish between such a manifestation of psychopathy as opposed to that of narcissism? The therapist's experience of the narcissist will include a registration that he, the therapist, might just as well not be in the room, for all his personhood matters to the narcissist. The psychopath, on the other hand, is adept at giving the other a sense that he is important to the subject. I can think of two other such cases that I have dealt with: one other unaware, the second with a realization after only a few sessions, but still without being able to hold on to the patient.

Both Don and Phil, like Manny, were self-referred when they feared that they were at grave risk of losing their spouses.

Don presented as a needy little boy, though he was a successful businessman. He seemed keen on having my approval and on gaining my advice. I believe that many psychopaths who seek treatment at such junctures in their lives do so with the belief that they can mine the gold of the therapist's bag of tricks and be able to use these tricks, or "tools" as they themselves would call them, to better manipulate their spouses to stay with them, and to do so without having to forge any psychostructural change in themselves at all. Don would be weepy, and I would have the false impression that he was establishing rapid trust and dependence. This is quite different than Jacques or Matt, each of whom had deep and genuine needs to fuse with the analyst. Don continued on for about six months. I do remember a visiting instructor from New York hearing something of this case and telling me that my patient was a psychopath; unfortunately, I was not able to utilize this communication at that time. At any rate, once Don had his wife back, and was fairly certain that he could keep her, he left treatment, leaving me with that same feeling Manny had, that I had had the stuffing knocked out of me.

Phil was another psychopath who presented in crisis over the departure of his wife and children. Phil had been recently diagnosed ADD and wrote off many of his historical and repetitive relationship difficulties to this, which he considered a medical problem now under control with medication. He even attributed much of his violence, which he did not identify as violence, to his ADD. He was very bright, a highly trained professional, and was able to espouse an understanding of the need for long-term depth-oriented treatment. His cannibalistic avarice, his efforts to extract from others whatever he desired, with concern for impact on them based solely on his need to maintain his oral-erotic supplies—these very soon became manifest in the transference. However, he gave me little chance to deal with him, I suspect because of his fear that I had his number and was thus an enemy to be vanquished by whatever means.

Psychopaths have long been seen as a bane of psychotherapy. Batterer psychopaths are equally elusive. I believe that, with further experience, reflection, study, and supervision, I will get better at dealing with this population, indeed, that I have already, and that in time I may be able to keep them in treatment where analysis can then do its work. Currently, it may well be that the modern school of psychoanalysis is making some strides in this area, especially at the Boston Graduate School of Psychoanalysis's Center for the Study of Violence.

QUESTIONS OF TECHNIQUE

Let me return to the case of Pablo as a case in which to examine technique. Was I then too biased in the direction of favoring the narcissistic transference? Were my supervisors similarly biased at that time? Would the founder of modern psychoanalyis have found my interpretations of and interventions pursuant to this patient's narcissistic transference as consonant with his clinical and theoretical intentions? In these regards, did I fail to interpret enough, based on a too narrow view that one does not interpret when a narcissistic transference is characterologically unresolved? Should this tenet only apply to a restraint from interpretation when the afflicted ego is in ascendency in the moment? Might many patients who demonstrate a good deal of narcissistic defense nonetheless be best served by a technique that allows for a sophisticated grasp and deployment of interpretation? Did I therefore fail to ally myself with and address myself sufficiently to his observing ego?

Specifically, I retrospectively question the following. Had I been able to follow the patient's free associations, to notice the foreclosures of same, and to respond interpretively based on the finest deployment of object relations and classical theory, while avoiding their pitfalls and still deploying the best of modern psychoanalytic methods, would I have kept him through a full life of treatment?

On the other hand, I must also consider how much my self-doubts are not the conscious manifestations of narcissistic countertransference. How much are my doubts reflecting his? In the narcissistic countertransference we may experience that which is disavowed by our patient, and experience it in such a way that we assume their feeling, attitude, etc. as our own when, in truth, it is our patient's, which is induced in us. In this case, how much was my patient assessing himself as a failure in the analysis, that no matter how hard he tried he could not get it right for me? Might he have felt that eventually, no matter how hard he tried, no matter what successes he had with me or in my eyes, I nonetheless would ultimately abandon him? In fact, at times during his more contentious periods in the analysis he had interrupted his onslaughts to ask me how it was that I had not gotten rid of him yet. The very inclusion of "yet" in his question seems to indicate that he expected that I indeed would eventually get around to rejecting him. So why shouldn't he have gotten rid of me before I got rid of him? After all, he feels very "gotten rid of" by his parents but has not been able to arrive at any emotional acceptance of or peace with who they are. He appears a long way from being able to genuinely grieve for what he will never have, what he has always longed for. I expect that his grief is of the same unbearable quality as that of Jacques, and that he resists it mightily for that very reason. Accepting the great damage in these patients, the helplessness and hopelessness that it is incumbent upon us to endure if we are to work well with them, makes this work something not for all of us.

Ultimately, as Margolis (1979) reminds us, joining techniques, first and foremost, find their greatest efficacy in their utility developing and evolving the narcissistic transference. Thus, with the greatest clarity of the cases in my experience, joining techniques were necessary with Jacques in order to interest him in treatment, in order to move him along through many and long-lived narcissistic transference times during which an interpretive posture would have felt to him at its best an experience of privation that he would have brooked only for so long. I believe there are many batterers who present themselves in treatment, early on and sometimes for long periods, in much the same need of joining techniques, or else they will not give us a second glance. This would be much the same as Aichhorn's delinquents being caught in his spin of narcissistic transference space, in the lack of which these young patients would not have given Aichhorn a second glance as well. And then there is a wide variety of joining technique types, and some of us will be better with some than with others. Or better with certain patient types than others. Or more able to intuit the treatment needs of some of them more than others. We will have to work harder with some recurring batterer presentation types than others, as, for example, is the case for myself with psychopathic batterers, whereas I believe there are analysts and therapists who intuitively know more about how to work with them. And knowing when to shift to a more traditional psychoanalytic posture, and being well trained in both, the latter requisite probably being exceedingly rare, is also going to be of paramount importance if we are to be able to carry many batterers through full psychoanalytic voyages, as Joyce McDougall (1995) is fond of calling them.

It is the work inside the transference-countertransference matrix/relationship wherein the battle for cure will be lost or won. This point, and its attendant demands upon the analyst, generates many hard-won lessons, seemingly with boundless vicissitudes. When working with the preverbal patient, joining techniques (here used in the broadest sense to encompass all those techniques that bypass the observing ego and "speak" directly to the afflicted ego [Geltner 1995]) constitute our only adequate means of reaching our patient in meaningful ways—as much so as nonreasoning modes of communication constitute our only communication with the preverbal child. Yet, with batterer patients, we will be sorely tempted again and again to fail to heed this knowledge (Scalia 1994).

With our preverbal patients we must tolerate a great deal of uncomfortable knowledge about them while we are helping them gain the strength to begin to explore such material, such parts of themselves. We must then forego what would be a self-serving act of confrontation or interpretation. Conversely, we must be clear-minded about the times when an interpretation or confrontation may be useful, and might in fact be grossly negligent to fail to provide. And we must try not to be seduced by our own wishes into believing that joining needed now indicates joining needed later, that interpretation now means interpretation rather than joining later.

As for countertransference—it must never be overlooked as a great possible indicator. At times countertransference is the very source of information on which a successful intervention turns. Or even on which a whole case might turn.

With batterers, given their greater propensity to resort to violence than our other preverbal patients, I myself have found the demands upon my person to be greater. The push for discharge through some type of motor activity, even a spitting out of words or an evacuation of their cannibalistic fears by projecting them into us (even without our consciously registering such fears)—as opposed to speaking with meaning, as opposed to freely associating and expressing meaning symbolically—in these patients is great. And, through induced feelings and attendant countertransference identifications (Racker 1968) with the patient or their objects (internal and external), this push for discharge will be greater within us than that which we experience with most other patients. In fact, mightn't this be one of the reasons our literature has a dearth of coverage of this population? How often do we unwittingly drive these patients out of treatment before even recognizing that they are patients who batter? Of course, we do this at times by acting out our inductions in ways assured to damage the treatment, but perhaps more often—certainly more insidious—is our avoiding registration of the most noxious countertransference experiences, such as the cannibalistic affective experiences I had of the patient Phil discussed briefly in this chapter.

CHAPTER NINE
WORKING THROUGH: A SYNTHESIS

A number of critical theoretical constructs have been reviewed throughout the body of this work. In terms of our understanding the patient's battering, key among them are narcissistic equilibrium/disequilibrium; symbiosis, separation-individuation, and the defenses against problematic and overwhelming developmental failures pursuant to these epochs; the senses of core and subjective self and disruptions especially in the sense of core self; the quintessential and prerequisite defense of *identification with the aggressor*. Key among the reviewed concepts that pertain to treatment are countertransference, transference, joining techniques, confrontation, and interpretation.[1]

In this closing chapter I will attempt to demonstrate how we must alternatingly apply these concepts within a given case and review three treatment cases in an effort to give a woven and experience-near explication of the concepts to the reader. *Working through* is classically understood to be "the psychological work which occurs after an insight has been given and which leads to a stable change in behavior and attitude" (Greenson 1967), a kind of work understood to occur during analysis of solid ego structures. But as our work here focuses more on narcissistic resistances and transferences, working through might also be understood as the analyst repeatedly containing projective identifications and other inductions of the patient, silently interpreting, as Thomas Ogden (1982) puts it, and joining/mirroring until such time as the patient begins to oscillate between narcissistic and object transference states, at which latter times the classical conceptualization of working through, along with its interpretive work, becomes relevant.

A reminder. There is great pressure on psychotherapists today to provide quick and overtly demonstrable treatment outcomes, after the fashion of managed care treatment conceptualizations, in the manner that Michael Szollosy (1998) calls a deontologizing of the subject, in his "Winnicott's Potential Spaces: Using Psychoanalytic Theory to Redress the Crises of Postmodern Culture," a paper presented at the 1998 Modern Language Association Convention in San Francisco. While the pressure derives from managed care and insurance companies, on the one hand, it behooves us to wonder at our complicity, for without sufficient therapist acquiescence to these incursions it is doubtful that a thing like managed mental health care could exist. Even as we are change agents for our culture, so are we also reflections and products of that same culture that deontologizes the subject. Ironically, one often finds a greater bastion of psychoanalysis today in university humanities studies than in psychology, counseling, social work, or psychiatry departments.

There appear to be universal resistances to the very act of doing depthwork with batterers. Who wants to accept how little change we must often content ourselves with! Who wants to be faced with the inevitable questions these patients leave us as to our treatment efficacy! Or have to accept ambiguous successes and failures, often decidedly incomplete analyses! And our human or existential imperfections may be easily underscored or indicated in this work. Embarrassing accentuations of our character foibles will occur because of the pressures inherent in the transference-countertransference matrix with batterers. And we must be ready to accept that we will come across sometimes glaring blindnesses that we have maintained with one or another patient for some time during our evolving treatment of them. Racker's "Even as we are adults and analysts, so too are we infants and neurotics" comes to mind again. We must strive toward being the "sage psychoanalyst," as Robert Marshall (1994) referred to Benjamin Margolis, while continually striving to recognize our necessarily lifelong student selves.

JACQUES

A further look at Jacques's life history is in order. He was born to a mixed race couple—his mother white and his father Native American—both parents being deeply engaged in and identified with a criminal lifestyle, especially prostitution and drug dealing. His first year of life is reported to have been characterized by psychological and physical neglect, emotional and physical abuse, and possibly infant sexual abuse, by potentially more than one pedophile.

Most important, a great deal of severe domestic violence existed in his parents' marriage, Jacques doubtless having been directly exposed to much of it. A homicidal pall permeated the familial atmosphere, manifested in the father in ways that may have included an extrafamilial murder and that did include a self-inflicted, Russian roulette gunshot to his head, which left him permanently and severely debilitated.

Jacques's mother has a life-threatening drug and alcohol addiction that has progressively occupied her life from at least her early teens. It will likely kill her, and, indeed, almost has now, on at least several occasions. Jacques has been exposed to the worst of this as well.

When he was two years old, he and his mother and two younger sisters (neither the half-sister mentioned in the last chapter – these sisters being his mother's offspring by yet another man) made an interstate move with Johnny, the man who would eventually stab Jacques nearly to death. This move was ostensibly a rescue of the mother from an abusive relationship, and from drugs and alcohol.

Of the four, only Jacques had the physical appearance of being non-Caucasian, precipitating many years' worth of crude and dehumanizing racial epithets heaped upon Jacques by Johnny. He was called "half-breed," "Injun," "redface," "squaw girl." He was singled out for all sorts of abuse, his mother and sister receiving far less than he. In fact, the mother appears not only to have avoided confronting her husband with his maltreatment of her son but also to have unconsciously supported it.

One incident that stands out: at about age eight a nut had vibrated loose from a bolt on the lawnmower with which Jacques had just mowed the lawn. Johnny blamed Jacques for this and forced him to search in vain for it for hours. He was not even allowed inside until nightfall, which would have been late in our northern latitudes summer. Powerlessness, hatred, and shame were brewing strongly for him in that emblematic incident. Another event: Johnny regularly "inspected" Jacques's dresser drawers to determine whether Jacques had "properly" folded his clothes. If not, all the clothes were dumped onto the floor for refolding. This series of self-identifying moments carries an accumulation of helplessness, rage, and shame. Yet another time: once when Johnny arrived home late at night and found that Jacques had left a television out of place, he pulled his sleeping stepson from his bed, threw him on the floor, threw his own body on top of Jacques's and repeatedly punched him in the face. I recall Jacques's telling me of this event with a partial measure of detachment, though that telling was long before the depressive period I discussed in the previous chapter.

There were simply countless incidents of psychological and physical abuse. Throughout it all, his mother "stood by her man," even after her husband almost killed her son. His "blueprinting" for homicidal violence with himself as the perpetrator, through identification with the aggressor, became all that much greater. To make matters even worse, when his mother was not "standing by her man," one of her typical ways of interacting with her son, and one of her typical ways of trying to soothe him, was to behave quite seductively with him, and I do mean quite blatantly seductively. She presented much of the *malignant hysteric* (Bollas 2000) and gave him the internalized sense that exhibitionistic sexuality was the best maternal soothing available, constituted the best of what might be one's *internal mother*, which became very clear in his exploitation of girls and of sexuality. What an overall recipe for disaster!

Degrading verbal abuse was commonplace. Chronic, unrelenting, lower-grade physical abuse was a given. The mother's blaming of Jacques for it was also a constant.

When he was fourteen years old, he blatantly defied his stepfather, refusing to comply with a command the stepfather had issued. Johnny threatened to hurl his "throwing knife" at him, but still received no compliance. Fancying himself a great knife man, he tossed his treasured implement at his son of twelve years and sunk the blade in his back, puncturing a lung and dropping him to the ground instantly. Jacques remembers his mother expressing, first, horror but immediately recovering and beginning to plot how she would protect her husband from the police—as her son lay there dying! Indeed, his heart did stop beating on the short ambulance ride to the hospital.

The reader will recall the following: my response to his early cockiness and dismissiveness and to his self-reports of his sadism, especially his tormenting a young girl on the school bus, his depression when I was called in to the group home at his request, my response to his explosiveness and intimidation in the group home. Other relevant case experiences follow.

On our trip to the winter hills above town, he told me of suicidal ideation as response to the unbearable feelings he endured regarding his lost childhood.[2] The pain of this is manifest in his fantasy of a Christmas holiday! And the time when I had been called in to the group home late at night for him, and his pain was palpable, all but absolutely unbearable—when such pain cannot be transformed through the medium of a relationship in which the analyst other receives its affective wording, as in Jacques's case, what happens to it? Does the pain itself become the primary transformational object, to be sought out for solace? Like the boy in Sharon Olds's "Leaving the Island," does he have to shroud himself in a blanket of unbearable pain in order to feel the presence of an internal mother, or of an internal father? Does he have to put that experience into another in order to do so? Did he internalize enough of good-enough experiences with his analyst to alter such a horrific course? Is the answer somewhere in between? Must he cause great harm to others and himself and struggle with competing representations, now being gratified by hurting another, later suffering guilt for it?

He was aware of how close he "walked on the edge"—that was his vernacular for it—and would often explore with me, at his own initiation, just how close he might presently be to plummeting over that edge. When he expressed his recurring fantasies of murdering peers whom he deemed dismissive and persecutory, I would often have to join him in a variety of ways, but especially in the two following ones.[3] I would be sure to join him in his experience of outrage at being psychologically persecuted, allowing him ample opportunity to experience attendant powerful affects through talking with me, thereby obviating or at least attenuating his need to act out his violent fantasies. When this response was insufficient to ameliorate the affect's push for discharge, I would respond much as I had to his description of taunting the little girl on the bus—basically "outcrazying the patient" (Spotnitz 1985). Often, then, he would close with a summation that included the folly of ever acting out such fantasies, as that would indeed be a plummeting over the edge, and in fact a landing in prison, much like his stepfather and an uncle who is in prison for murder. At other times, I was left with a nagging uncertainty about his stability, doubtless a reflection of his own subjective experience. Isn't it ironic, and a terrible testament to the power of both the repetition compulsion and identification with the aggressor, that he flirts with ideas of knifing and shooting people!? The blueprint for him to enact violent crime is so strongly imprinted that it is amazing he had not killed someone.

I have discussed his sexual violence in previous chapters and will add here only that I am aware of other such incidents; he considers himself at risk of taking sexual advantage of those weaker than himself, including younger children, harking back, through identification with the aggressor, to his own early victimizations as well as merely reflecting the overall unsettling reality that his libidinal and aggressive drives are far from contained, can easily run amok, and are readily discharged without consideration for others, in efforts to stabilize a violently disrupted narcissistic equilibrium.[4]

As I have stated, one of my most obvious errors with him was during his stay at the group home, when he would be indignant at my leaving to go home. "Sure! Go ahead! Go home to your family!" Or just after a group therapy session, which would constitute his only contact with me on a given day: "What! You're going home?! You just got here!" And these were strongly emotional communications, which I may well have been able to utilize to his greater advantage had I understood more then about the management of negative transference. I might have been able to give him a transference-countertransference container for his rage. It is also quite likely that he was merely not ready enough to give up more than small and momentary pieces of his idealizing and twinship transference to me at that time. In the latter case the difficult reality of accepting the highly protracted nature of such cases' narcissistic resistances becomes highlighted.

When I left the group home, after only nine months, the organization became unable to provide a safe enough external net while concomitantly honoring this young man's need for narcissistic resistances. Instead, too much confrontation, without making him feel safe and understood at the same time, became the order of the day. Within a few months, with his stay at the home feeling now like an absurd infringement on his personal rights, he convinced the organization and the state to emancipate him, allowing him to move out of state with his stepmother and half-sister, as I have discussed in chapter 8.

There was another treatment stage, however, before he left Montana. I arranged a series of family therapy sessions with his mother and stepfather.[5] His mother attended only two of these sessions, then disappeared, her histrionics dominating her during the sessions and after her departure from them entering heavy bouts with alcohol and drugs. Johnny came to town with his counselor from the state prison's pre-release center, which was by then his home. The mother's volatility in these sessions contrasted with the stepfather's presentation—he seeming relatively present. Though he claimed that the knifing was partly accidental—saying that he had meant to stick the knife into the post right next to Jacques—he did accept responsibility for a lot of physical and emotional abuse. There was a good deal of connection between them, on the one hand, while, on the other, Jacques was left with an overwhelming sense of futility in his wish to somehow vanquish his stepfather, a motive underlying his adamant requests for these sessions, as Johnny did not present himself as the "animal" Jacques had expected. His frustration during the sessions was equally compounded by Johnny's limited ability to empathize with Jacques's experiences of victimization at his hands. A psychopath? A narcissist? Any sincerity in his efforts to reach out to Jacques? At any rate, Jacques did get to be in the same room with him, with me (and all I represented to him) in attendance.

I continued sessions with him on the phone for about six months before his stepmother pulled the plug on him. But I am left with an incomplete close to the case. He would have continued, I am quite certain, to the natural close of his psychoanalytic voyage, had the state held itself responsible to see him through what it had financially supported for four years. But the state cut him off at eighteen. That was that!

As I moved through my work with him, it was often necessary to honor the preverbal nature of his situation. That is, so much of his experience of his life was centered around an easily and violently disruptable narcissistic equilibrium, which would plunge him into emergency or acute psychic survival situations. Also, so much of his quotidian life was characterized by achieving gratification through his identification with the aggressor. His split off and expelled or projected experiences of victimization were routinely placed into others. Of course, he initially had no idea that he was executing any such defense of himself. His capacity for empathy, his ability to perceive and imagine the separate and unique personhoods of fellow human beings was obviously terribly impaired early on. His need to experience other-excluding symbiotic states was very high in the beginning, and may still be quite a problem, though obviously with significant attenuation possible, from situation to situation.

Observing ego around these matters was nonexistent when we began to work together, and thus all of my initial work with him had to be focused on making myself an object of interest to him, and later on salving a terribly "afflicted" ego. His narcissistic transference had to develop and then evolve. In his case I had to present a glorified image of an amalgamation of myself and of him—reminiscent of Aichhorn's work with juvenile delinquents—thus giving him cause to find interest in me, so that he could feel that I had something to offer him, that I was not another mere white, middle-class, sheltered excuse for a man. To this end, I first established myself as undaunted by his brazen sadistic exhibitionism, and as even keenly interested in it, even perhaps as more skilled at or comfortable with sadism than he. I then also accentuated for him my already self-evident athleticism, which I could see that he admired, while simultaneously, though only covertly at first, presenting myself as not only strong but also gentle. Additionally, I attended well to giving ungrudgingly affective validation to the psychically heroic aspects of him that were already in evidence upon our first meeting, which I genuinely admired. For example, his insights about others' fears of their own instinctual lives were often quite to the point and accurate. I would exuberantly agree with him. Or his ironic wishes for social justice in the world were of a heroic character also, his being willing to endure any hardship if only he could bring about such justice. At such times, I would comment on his ideational courage with unconcealed admiration. These were doubtless his first experiences of being deeply appreciated for his inner life, for his true self (Winnicott), for his personal idiom (Bollas), as I do believe these were, though skewed, expressions of what he was born with.

After some time he began to demonstrate curiosity about himself—his potential in life, obstacles to his success—and he began to be troubled by his sadistic and dismissive treatment of others. As I had become a firmly entrenched selfobject for him, he was especially was troubled by his intensely hostile and potentially violent treatment of me in the group home incident described. He took on an enduring interest in exploring how he came to be who he is, and how he might grow more into his potential. He was especially concerned that he himself not become an abusive parent, understanding the pitfalls he faced in that regard. He'd become capable of grappling with confrontations and interpretations, of calling upon observing ego, while feeling sufficiently unafflicted to do so.

How might one understand that I identified over time very strongly with some of his feelings of victimization? This often took the form of my feeling strong indignation at what I (probably correctly) deemed to be very poor and at times inflammatory treatment of him by other adults in attendance. The intensity of my feelings were doubtless, as they unconsciously were for him, a reflection of his disavowed feelings of overwhelming victimization by and disappointment in his parents. I felt not only great compassion for him—not even only indignation at the past and present abuses of him—but also strong wishes to parent him, to nurture him, to give him a combination in myself of the mother and father he had deserved but been denied. At times I imagined what it would be like were he my son. Is this Spotnitz's *anaclitic countertransference*, in which the analyst develops feelings for the patient that the patient's parents should have had for him but didn't? Doubtless, Jacques registered, on some level, these feelings and fantasies within me. I expect this was also a function of our shared pleasure at defeating so much destructive force within him, a function of the team effort we generated.

PABLO

Pablo found his parents rejecting his wife from the beginning of their marriage. For years he participated with them in blaming her for whatever "unpleasure" needed attribution. Perhaps he especially helped create this team blaming when he felt someone needed blaming for his struggles. He had until then never challenged his idealized views of his parents, or the family inculcations of paternal authoritarianism and rejections of psychological-mindedness and affective life. By the time he reached treatment, in his thirties, he was ripe for challenging mores that were already reaching their integrity-breaking point. He soon began to examine values and beliefs that were oppressing him and his wife and children.

When I question my culpability in his precipitous termination of treatment, I am reminded that although I did treat him for ten years of weekly sessions, this would equal only about two and a half or three years of daily sessions in a classical format. But I get ahead of myself. While I believe that some good interpretive work was done over the years, it seems to me that the bulk of our important work was in a preverbal arena, and specifically within the confines of the narcissistic transference (Spotnitz 1987; Kohut 1972).

I believe that within the transference he moved through a symbiotic pervasiveness in his life. He appears to have entered more fully a separation-individuation phase of ego development, but unfortunately he could not simultaneously experience me as safe when his relationship to me reached this plane. His sense of core self remains highly vulnerable, I fear, as he continues to negotiate a world shadowed by objects where the internal mother and father of separation are now considered so unsafe and so toxic that he could not continue to experience them at all in his transference connection to me. He felt that I had suddenly become as oppressive of his self-continuity as he experienced his father to be. No amount of sensitivity on my part to these issues mattered at all. Nor did insistent interpretation touch him. Rather he was insistent that I was oppressive and incapable of understanding him. And this after many years of his feeling deeply and gratefully understood by me. In fact, it was only when I conveyed to him my understanding and acceptance of his leaving that it seemed utterly important to him that he part from me. It was only then that he again felt understood and grateful, and then that he was able to terminate with a safe feeling, with a warm attitude toward and warm experience of me.

My countertransference was of helplessness, and of being murdered. That is a strong sense, a strong statement, I am aware, and I do not make it lightly. And, in fact, it is consonant with what we know of his transference antecedents, as most obviously manifest in the death of his twin brother. In fact, these feelings must pervade my patient's life or unconscious psychostructural substrate, lying in wait, as it were, to be activated unawares for the patient and his external objects. This structure must have been active when he made his physically ailing father suffer a psychic disowning by him just days before his precipitous termination with me. Was he manically cleaning house, omnipotently triumphing over those he longed for, but which longing he had to repudiate (Klein 1940)? His father had traveled far to visit him, traveled in poor health. Both parents were reported to be in failing health and were nearing the ends of their lives. Pablo had already more or less cut them off relationally and had kept them in limbo about their status with him for a few years. He was intent upon revenge, intoning "Payback's a bitch!" He visited with his father for five hours at a hotel, during which time his father made a plea for his return to convivial relations with the family. Pablo heard him out and rebuffed him in the end. He perceived his now enfeebled father's efforts as cold-hearted and still authoritarian, thus worthy of harsh rejection. He felt his father's efforts were too little, too late.

He is trapped in a need to defeat his father, to make him suffer for all real and phantasied disappointments, violations, slights.[6] No stone must go unturned! His insistence on justice has run amok. I worry that his guilt for his vengeful and persecutory behavior toward and attitudes about his parents, a guilt that is largely unconscious, will itself persecute him, yielding brutal superego attacks upon him. He has also seriously damaged his inner objects, crystallizing representations of them as he characterized his parents, and he will have to thereby suffer loneliness and worry about retaliation from a world he has generated as unequivocally persecutory, as brooking no ambivalence, as allowing no human fallibility. Having no analyst through whom to process any of this, and indeed having similarly destroyed at least a large part of the internalized analyst, may have terribly destructive consequences.

Was it a foregone conclusion that he was going to ultimately defeat the analyst in this way? Will I ever know?[7]

MATT

Matt has been moving into a more pronounced object transference, appearing to usher in a treatment-destructive possibility, a time in which his presenting symptoms are under control, he is very pleased about his ability to hold, contain, reflect upon his anger and not allow himself or others to be mercilessly buffeted about by it. He appears to have developed a more secure sense of core self and is not so threatened by "unthinkable anxieties" that hitherto could only be defended against by identification with the aggressor. And even when he experiences anxiety on a core self level, he is able to provide himself some calming reflection and undoubtedly an unconscious conjuring up of his analyst as an accepting, reflective, noncensorious object. But how solidified are such gains, and can he endure the rigors of an object transference and of further separation-individuation that will call on him to find solace in progressively greater capacities to be alone? Will he need to flee treatment?

One and a half years after the paragraph above was written, Matt has continued treatment, as I have mentioned previously. He is still vulnerable, but is now more cognizant of his vulnerability and more tolerant of enduring its articulation.

We as a field of psychoanalytic explorers may not be in a position to answer many of our questions yet. Perhaps some of the crucial questions are not yet formulated. Analytic treatment of this group is sparse. However, I hope that my efforts will provide further spark for psychotherapists and psychoanalysts alike to more fully consider a necessary depth inquiry of this population.

I hope I have given a thumbnail sketch of salient and germane concepts of import to understanding and treating batterers, at least from the vantage point of our current states of knowledge, wisdom, and analytic capacities.

I also hope to have not only inspired some further analytic interest in batterers but to have given cause for wonder about where intimate violence might be concealed from our clinical observation.

These patients are often passionate individuals who will offer unique opportunities for engagement both narcissistically and analytically. They can be both infuriatingly tedious and inspirationally courageous, repellent and endearing. They challenge our notions of analyzability. They are not as a group the monsters that we have all too often depicted them to be. The prevalence of intimate violence mandates that we take the more complex look at batterers that is now beginning to occur.

APPENDIX

THE POWER AND CONTROL WHEEL

PHYSICAL **VIOLENCE** SEXUAL

USING COERCION AND THREATS
Making and/or carrying out threats to do something to hurt her • threatening to leave her, to commit suicide, to report her to welfare • making her drop charges • making her do illegal things

USING INTIMIDATION
Making her afraid by using looks, actions, gestures • smashing things • destroying her property • abusing pets • displaying weapons.

USING ECONOMIC ABUSE
Preventing her from getting or keeping a job • making her ask for money • giving her an allowance • taking her money • not letting her know about or have access to family income.

USING EMOTIONAL ABUSE
Putting her down • making her feel bad about herself • calling her names • making her think she's crazy • playing mind games • humiliating her • making her feel guilty.

POWER AND CONTROL

USING MALE PRIVILEGE
Treating her like a servant • making all the big decisions • acting like the "master of the castle" • being the one to define men's and women's roles

USING ISOLATION
Controlling what she does, who she sees and talks to, what she reads, where she goes • limiting her outside involvement • using jealousy to justify actions.

USING CHILDREN
Making her feel guilty about the children • using the children to relay messages • using visitation to harass her • threatening to take the children away

MINIMIZING, DENYING AND BLAMING
Making light of the abuse and not taking her concerns about it seriously • saying the abuse didn't happen • shifting responsibility for abusive behavior • saying she caused it.

PHYSICAL **VIOLENCE** SEXUAL

NOTES

INTRODUCTION

1. This allegiance never waned even when the stepfather finally left the scene and Puck's mother continued to disappoint and disillusion him in a variety of ways; always the disillusionment was transferred onto other figures. Additionally, Puck should not be confused with Jacques, who appears later in the book and who shares with Puck a good deal of similar family history and similar maladjustments to it.

2. Unfortunately, when I left the treatment center he rapidly returned to his successfully intimidating ways and soon had to be transferred to another psychiatric hospital. There he was again physically violent and was frequently physically restrained. Sadly, his path then followed the revolving door pattern in which he was unmanageable everywhere he went. He solidified a societally disenfranchised identity and finally ended up in state prison at nineteen.

3. To my way of thinking, *tactics* is a misnomer inasmuch as it implies a conscious and cognizant effort, which is often simply not the case.

4. Indeed, since completion of the first draft of this book, I have become aware of some psychoanalytic contributions other than my own two earlier papers, such as Fonagy (1999); Dutton (1998); Celani (1994); these works in some ways corroborate my own views, while respectively neglecting treatment concerns, making salient elisionary psychoanalytic errors, or, ironically, through a rather doctrinaire pronouncement of untreatability, projecting into the batterer the same unequivocal heinousness and false criminalization that I perceive in Duluth.

1. AFFECT REGULATION AND NARCISSISTIC EQUILIBRIUM

1. One might fruitfully wonder what these walls could have represented of his internal object world.

2. Is it possible to name or conceptualize this space in a way unique to the batterer or the pervert? In fact, it is perversion that has him in prison right now. I imagine that the pervert appropriates, in lieu of an unavailable transitional space, a *perverse space* that 1. demands a rigidly controlled internal and external world and 2. serves to fend off psychotic anxieties and disintegration.

3. *Object* and *other* are sometimes used synonymously, even by psychoanalytic writers. Yet they are distinctly different signifiers. Briefly, "other" can be understood as an actual other person, an external person, a person in the real. Our registration of this other is always subject to our personalizing it—or what Grotstein (2000) calls *autochthonizing*—now justifying the signifier object. "Object" is a more multiple concept than this, however, signifying 1. actual others, 2. internalized or introjected others, 3. any object of the subject's experience, be it a person, a piece of music, a recurrent thought, our autochthonized versions of these. One may speak of "internal objects" and "external objects."

4. We might wonder how much our batterer patients' difficulties with affect regulation and narcissistic equilibrium, and especially with these functions' resistances to growth, do not coexist with concomitant physiological or neurological deficits or impairments of some sort, albeit psychologically reparable neurological phenomena.

2. THE EXPERIENCE OF SELF AND OTHER

1. Stern's work describes experience-near material of the patient's world. It is of the stuff of phenomena, rather than noumena, of empiricism rather than rationalism. In Grotstein's (2000) vernacular, we could say that it addresses the *phenomenal subject* but does not attend to the *ineffable subject of the unconscious*. Although Mahler's work begins with empirical data, she quickly becomes highly inferential in both what she believes she is observing and in what she is concluding. There are abysmal divergences within psychoanalysis these days over such differences, and, rather than attempting to elucidate any of these, or their implications, I will simply draw from both. I find Stern's work to nearly articulate much of the batterer's more conscious and preconscious experience, while Mahler's is closer to the *thing*ness of the unconscious. Both are highly useful in understanding batterers, and in establishing and maintaining treatment alliances with them.

2. One is here reminded of Winnicott's views of the mother in her functions as transitional object and total environment in the infant's experience (1992). Bollas's *transformational object* (1987) also comes to mind.

3. The reader may wish to note that such terms as the *co-created* just used actually have great theoretical and clinical implications as elucidated in different schools

of psychoanalytic thought. When I first wrote the above words, I had no such sensibility. Attempting to account for this now by altering the text is not feasible and in its subtlety is probably not germane to most readers.

4. During a time of far too infrequent sessions, he managed to report, to his considerable chagrin, that he had forcefully pushed his wife, after more than two years of absolutely no violence. If he can manage to find the resources to see me with even a modicum of frequency, such outbursts become more possibly containable.

5. Though Jacques was to later develop the capacity for significant empathy, he has still not developed the ability to sublimate his considerable libidinal and aggressive drives, as treatment was disrupted too early.

6. For an explication of the *terminal object,* see Bollas's essay, "Preoccupation Unto Death" in *Cracking Up* (1995).

7. While it can be argued that recent infant research challenges much of Mahler's work, insofar as it was inferential and noumenal, much of it remains unchallengeable by phenomenological arguments. And Mahler's work, like Klein's, still proves to be of significant clinical usefulness.

8. While some may argue the validity of the idea of putting experience into another, such that the other experiences the actual disavowed contents of the projector, we can instead consider the mechanism of transmission being something more like the following. The projector violently expels a part of itself, and will cannily search for avenues in the recipient wherein the expelled contents might coincide with the recipient's vulnerabilities. That is, the projector unconsciously seeks to activate in the recipient the mental form or content that the projector wants to be rid of but that ordinarily resides in the recipient as well, now being prodded by the projector. Grotstein (2000, personal communication) points out that the analyst does not have to "catch" the projective identification in order for it to have taken place. Projective identification is an intrasubjective process; it occurs entirely within the subject. When the analyst catches the projective identification, we ought to speak of an *introjective counteridentification* taking place in the analyst. This is important metapsychologically and clinically, as to miss this point goes hand in hand with a kind of watering down of psychoanalysis, wherein the weightiness of the unconscious is lost and analysis is seen as an interpersonal process that does not have to struggle with the noumenal at all, but only with the phenomenal, which would be a terrible sterilization of a rich enterprise. It essentially eliminates from study and engagement the *ineffable subject of the unconscious.*

9. In Betty Joseph's (1987), and other Kleinians', visceral vernacular.

10. Yet, paradoxically, we must consider here the notions of conservative and terminal object motives. That is, in brief, how much is the threat of an inability to find object constancy simultaneously a gratification along the lines of finding the origi-

nal impinging object who was nevertheless the primary object of attachment and desire and thus necessarily longed for? Therefore, when in a state of suffering with one's immediate object world, how much is one driven, unrecognizedly, to sustain that very suffering, insofar as it conjures up powerful returns to the lost one?

11. I am loosely referring to both Stern's and Kohut's contributions as self psychological.

3. IDENTIFICATION WITH THE AGGRESSOR

1. At this point in my analytic development, more than a year since that session, I wonder if what I've learned about detecting projective identifications in a patient's associations, coupled with when one can effectively (i.e., in a way digestible and appreciated by the patient) interpret them, might have allowed for Matt to recognize his culpability and responsibility at that time.

2. I do not recall, as it was immaterial to me and I may not have registered it, whether the father hit the boy with the knuckles of his fist or with the blunt face of it: many parents—in my clinical experience and extrapolating from it—consider these knuckle punches somehow not punches at all.

3. Victimology advocates sometimes point to the fact that not all people who were battered as children themselves become batterers as evidence that batterers batter because they are able to. This argument neglects the consideration of one's idiom and innate character style. One's core pathological fixations or complexes are only partly determined by one's history. And someone becoming obsessive or schizoid—which may go unnoticed by this argument—in partial response to a battered childhood is certainly not a greater achievement in adjustment necessarily than one whose battering is quite visible.

4. As incidental parenthesis, sensitized as I am of late to society's propagandizing of AD(H)D as biochemically caused, I would note that this particular boy will be a likely candidate to exhibit the behaviors we call ADHD, in his case most decidedly pursuant to such behavior by the father.

4. POLITICAL VERSUS CLINICAL DETERMINATION OF ABUSE AND OTHER ASSOCIATIONS

1. That is, as Bollas (1992) has elaborated, we may rationalize and seem to display a certain innocence that is actually a dissimulated violence toward the other.

2. In this regard, see chapter 7 on countertransference and induced psychic states.

3. The induction I am referring to is that defined by the modern school of psy-

choanalysis, and it is also one of the components of Thomas Ogden's exposition of projective identification. I will treat these issues in chapter 6. The work of James Grotstein and our conversations have brought me to question the exact mechanisms of said "induction" and the metapsychological and clinical implications of this point. I have referred to this in note 8, chapter 3, and cannot go into it further in this venue. But I will reiterate that this may be a matter of tremendous consequence for clinical practice, and even for the very continued existence of psychoanalysis. The crucial point has to do with "Can the other make us feel anything?" or is the experience of the other always necessarily mediated by our own projective identifications?

4. And here I do not mean intersubjective in its sense of the analytic school of thought by that name but rather in the sense of unconscious communication from one subject to another. Violations in the realm of the real will be capable of symbolic process by some and not by others. Thus one person will be traumatized by such a violation while another will not.

5. In this vein, see Richard Schur's *Countertransference Enactments* and Bollas's "The Fascist State of Mind" in his *Being a Character*. Schur explicates the way in which treatment centers routinely, practically universally, fail to recognize the countertransferences that are an inherent part of psychotherapy and instead act upon their patients in the very ways they are critical of their patients. Bollas's essay gives us an eloquent, psychodynamic depiction of the virtually quotidian existence and relative ubiquity of the interior life that allows fascism to flourish.

6. Yet it is not a given: it remains a possibility that she was hysterically or otherwise gratified by this action, rather than at all traumatized by it.

7. As is so often the case, I believe that to have made reliable differential diagnoses of either of these spouses would have required a knowledge of them that can only be acquired clinically through an unfolding and thoroughgoing psychoanalysis.

8. I would argue that the analyst or analytic therapist ought to have a *privilege*—much as clergy, attorneys, and journalists have sustained within their professions or vocations, while psychotherapists have forfeited theirs—to keep absolute patient confidentiality, thereby attempting to protect the integrity of the analytic or therapeutic space: see Bollas and Sundelson's *The New Informants*.

9. I believe that many will find the temptation to now consider her as borderline rather compelling. To my mind, we cannot sort out how much of what was then occurring was a function of Helen's psychic constitution as opposed to being secondary to and a consequence of her inability to maintain clear ego boundaries while under the pressures of two systems she found competing for her mentational allegiance: Hector and the shelter.

5. OUR UNWITTING PERSECUTION OF THE BATTERER AND OTHER FACILE CONVENIENCES

1. Indeed, as I have pointed out, even Celani (1994) has taken this position.

2. Curiously, equally flawed monothetic pathologizing used to be aimed at battered women, who were often diagnosed as borderlines, this given as the reason they stayed with battering husbands.

3. For an example and explication of this concept, see Christopher Bollas's "Borderline Desire" (1999), in *The Mystery of Things*, as well as his concept of the conservative object.

4. See Joseph Biden's "Violence Against Women: The Congressional Response," in the October 1993 *American Psychologist*.

5. Before press time, it has been pointed out to me that I can be read in places, here included, as implying that I see the women portrayed in this book as more weak-minded or gullible than the men. At this point, I can only deal with this in a note and state unequivocally that this is indeed *not* how I see it. I believe both spouses bring their own personal idioms, histories, strengths, and pathologies to these relationships.

6. See Christopher Bollas's "Violent Innocence" in his *Being a Character*.

6. COUNTERTRANSFERENCE

1. For excellent coverage of this vital topic across patient populations, see Marshall and Marshall (1988) and Schoenewolf (1993).

2. It should be noted that this definition, or even that of subjective countertransference, to be introduced below, does not include the purely transferential reactions of the therapist to his patient. This distinction puts one on difficult theoretical terrain.

3. Not to be understood in the contrived Alexandrian sense, but rather in the sense of naturally or spontaneously occurring junctures that the analyst manages in the direction of health and transformation.

4. Nonetheless, as Racker (1953:130) put it: "We are still children and neurotics even when we are adults and analysts." We sometimes can do no better than recognize after the fact that we have erred in word or deed through theretofore unrecognized countertransference.

5. It is perhaps a telling curiosity, however, that while we have criminalized spousal violence, we have not, unlike Sweden, for example, criminalized parental violence against children. We still allow for corporal punishment within certain levels of injurious consequence, much as domestic violence was once allowed. We still adopt a position that it is for the child's own good (Miller 1983).

6. In this vein, we would do well to keep in mind that, while physical strength differential is a factor in much domestic violence, greater strength is not a prerequisite for trauma-inducing capacity.

7. Again, a clarification: some adjudicated batterer patients either may need to be managed with the assistance of such invocation or may not belong in an outpatient group at all. Clearly, in the latter case especially, we must not forget that some of these patients are highly dangerous, and potentially so within the treatment setting.

8. At times, for economy of expression, the reader will have to infer that by *narcissistic patient* I mean narcissistic patients as well as pseudonarcissistic patients while their narcissistic defense is in ascendency.

9. Or again, as Grotstein points out, we may not have to catch it per se, as much as register it.

10. I think it is only fitting that, as stated elsewhere, this book has been written, in different eras, over a period in my professional development in which I have been exposed, more or less sequentially, to what sometimes seems to be incompatible psychoanalytic schools of thought. I cannot help but let these tensions in my thinking be apparent at any number of locations throughout the book. I would like to be able to present a more theoretically cohesive thesis, but I find that to be impossible at this point. Some of the theoretical tensions seem more ultimately resolvable to me, but, in thinking about batterers, practical clinical application is a problem when I try to harmonize some of my thinking. Part of the problem is that my practice has changed a great deal since the first draft of this book, such that at this writing I no longer see many batterer patients from whom to draw clinical and intervention data. I can only leave this problem a standing one and hope that others will take it up for the duration of their clinical caseloads with a preponderance of batterers. My reason for this insertion just now has to do with statements above regarding relational concerns in treatment, such as interaffectivity and intersubjectivity, and caveats about interpretation. Practically speaking, it now seems to me that there are times with preoedipal patients that a certain type of poised interpretation may be very beneficial, may be detrimental not to provide. There are controversies over the uses of *analytic space* and *free association* and the analyst's authority versus a more social constructivist view of a *relational* psychoanalysis, and they embody controversies over the dichotomizing of object versus narcissistic transferences. More practically speaking, with Lulu, did I have to *catch* so much of the patient's illness, or, in retrospect, based on what I have since learned of a quite respectful, authoritative, transformational-object type of interpreting, might I have spared her much labor based on what I know today? In fact, might her treatment have been far more effective? Of course, I cannot know the answers to those questions, but I nevertheless want them asked.

11. To follow up on note 10 above, as per my current comment on a necessary narcissistic countertransference, I will add my concerns wherever I find such statements inapplicable. In this case I believe the comment still relevant and correct, with the possible exception of the pseudonarcissistic type. Regarding this type of patient, my own disalignment of recent theoretical thinking and accretion of clinical experience makes me unable to venture much reliable information on that question.

12. Yet, such denial abounds in our culture. I do not fail to notice the likelihood that the following vignette may be representative of a fair portion of whoever reads this book. An officer of one of our national victim advocate organizations recently wrote me a letter addressing some of my views on countertransference acting out, which extends to child protection workers, of course. This officer told me, if I understood him correctly, that in his capacity as such a worker for many years he has not seen any mistreatment of individuals being investigated for abuse, he does not believe it happens, and I am mistaken if I think otherwise. Is denial a river in Africa?

13. Now, two years since his last violent incident, he painfully told me of a recent incident during which he pushed his wife, hard, and she had been hurt. He was quite ashamed—in contrast to the above-accounted earlier incident, which was given insouciantly.

7. TRANSFERENCE

1. See Marshall and Marshall (1988:184–186) for a sketch of the history and definition of the term *narcissistic transference.*

2. Indeed, though beyond the scope of this book, the question as to how much analytic theoreticians who do not utilize this concept might nonetheless be addressing similar phenomena in their schemata does arise. For example, in my own studies I am currently exploring this question within the contemporary works of André Green (e.g., *The Work of the Negative*) and of Christopher Bollas (e.g., *The Shadow of the Object*).

3. Let me clarify once again that I am not suggesting a coddling approach. There are other men I would confront in such a situation, to therapeutic end; Terry was not one of them.

4. André Green's "the negative," in his *The Work of the Negative.*

5. Of considerable significance, some few months after I wrote the above entry about the danger in his valuing the analyst, he told me this very thing—that it is very difficult for him to have me know that he feels any sense of need of me.

6. Indeed! In fact, his recent communication, mentioned in note 5, came upon the resolution of a threat by him to leave treatment very prematurely. It was not with

quite the cavalier attitude of Pablo, but it was delivered as though the analyst were of no consequence whatsoever.

8. JOINING TECHNIQUES

1. Robert Marshall's (1982) *Resistant Interactions: Child, Family, and Psychotherapist* offers the best accounting, of my acquaintance, for exemplifying what actually constitutes these modern psychoanalytic interventions.
My own 1998 essay gives a few other examples of these interventions with batterer patients.

2. See Marshall and Marshall (1988) for a review and schematic picture of transference and countertransference antecedents and consequents.

3. It should be noted that when I would thus join his resistance I would also offer similar intervention and support to his wife in her opposing position, thereby making it clear that I was not "taking sides" but instead able to understand both their points of view and that neither had to lose when the other was understood.

4. Doubtless, I provided him an external father, for introjection and identification, who could face his impulsiveness and destructiveness with affect-modulating and affect-containing articulated thought.

5. Not long after this intervention, and naively emboldened by its potent success, I ill-advisedly attempted a similar, though much milder intervention with another juvenile delinquent male, with whom I had *not* attended well to the need for a strong positive narcissistic transference as a prerequisite. Instead, I unrecognizedly used this intervention as the very gimmick I can now warn against. I lost that patient in that session. He never returned—nor should he have. Opportunities for this kind of intervention are very rare. I have utilized them only three times ever. And, as a final caveat, such an intense intervention should not be construed in a way to obscure the necessarily ubiquitous, much more subtle interventions that occur continuously throughout every analysis.

6. Consider, in this context, that he knew I had an investment in him that would make his running away a felt loss.

7. For a similar intervention in which an adolescent was fleeing and was grabbed by Carl Whitaker, see Napier and Whitaker's *The Family Crucible*. And, of course, see the writings of August Aichhorn for his allowing delinquent teens in residential treatment to exhaust their physical destructiveness in actual enactment.

8. Or, in retrospect, and being more fluent in Kleinian thought nowadays, was this rather a loosening of a previously strangleheld *manic position*, or manic defense? In this regard, see especially Klein (1935, 1940); and Winnicott (1935).

9. He is again in weekly sessions, beginning to pull it together in the real.

10. And, indeed, as I have noted, there has been a recent revival of violence, though now with a shame about it that had not hitherto existed.

9. WORKING THROUGH: A SYNTHESIS

1. I now believe that much more psychosexual material and object-relational material (both Kleinian and per the British independent school) must be explored. The use of free association and evenly suspended attentiveness and their elucidations of what unconscious mental contents are being acted out in battering, quite beyond though not to the exclusion of any narcissistic transference considerations, ought to be accentuated.

2. And, indeed, suicide and homicide remain risks in this young man's still untreated self, i.e., in a life in which treatment was interrupted and remains unavailable to him.

3. Joining seems to me, even retrospectively, to have been the intervention of choice, given the following. At these times, he was not to locate an observing ego through any interpretive effort on my part. He was embraced by, enthralled with, the notion—the keen affective edge—of killing some external(ized) persecutor. He was *held* by this conjuring, by this revenant of his inner world.

4. It must also be considered that for him pedophilia allows for an identification with the child as the same sexually loved person that he was, when his mother related so erotically to him. That is, pedophilia may resurrect his feelings of being soothed by his mother through her inappropriate sexual ministrations toward him.

5. We also had several phone sessions with his head-injured father, who lived in a separate domicile but in close contact with the stepmother Jacques was going to live with. These sessions served little purpose other than to verify what we already had been told, that his father was severely impaired cognitively, and presented himself as something of a hybrid between a grandiose narcissist and a mentally retarded child. So Jacques knew what he was getting into.

6. I employ the verb *phantasied* rather than *fantasied* here to underscore the Kleinian intrapsychic consideration of a "manic victory" over his sense of loss, of infantile psychic material blurring his objectivity about the sadness of this whole situation.

7. Indeed I may, as, just before press time, he has returned to treatment.

BIBLIOGRAPHY

Aichhorn, A. 1948. "Delinquency in a New Light." In O. Fleischmann, P. Kramer, and H. Ross, eds., *Delinquency and Child Guidance: Selected Papers.* New York: International Universities Press, 1964.

American Psychologist. 1993. 48, no. 10.

American Psychologist. 1999. 54, no. 1.

Betcher, T. and M. Ball. 1997. "Therapists' Awareness of Projective Identification and Identification with the Aggressor in the Therapeutic Relationship with the Batterer." Aurora University, Aurora, Illinois.

Bettelheim, B. 1974. *A Home for the Heart.* New York: Knopf.

Bollas, C. 1987. *The Shadow of the Object: Psychoanalysis of the Unthought Known.* New York: Columbia University Press.

—— 1992. *Being a Character: Psychoanalysis and Self Experience.* New York: Hill and Wang.

1995. *Cracking Up: The Work of Unconscious Experience.* New York: Hill and Wang.

—— 1999. *The Mystery of Things.* London and New York: Routledge.

—— 2000. *Hysteria.* London: Karnac.

Bollas, C. and D. Sundelson. 1995. *The New Informants: The Betrayal of Confidentiality in Psychoanalysis and Psychotherapy.* Northvale, N.J.: Aronson.

Bozeman Daily Chronicle. 2001. Bozeman, Montana, February 2.

Celani, D. 1994. *The Illusion of Love: Why the Battered Woman Returns to Her Abuser.* New York: Columbia University Press.

deMause, L. 1998. "The History of Child Abuse." *Journal of Psychohistory* 25, no. 3: 216–236.

Dutton, D. 1998. *The Abusive Personality: Violence and Control in Intimate Relationships.* New York: Guilford.

Eissler, K. 1949. "Some Problems of Delinquency." In K. Eissler, ed., *Searchlights on Delinquency*. New York: International Universities Press, 1949.

Fenichel, O. 1945. *The Psychoanalytic Theory of Neurosis*. New York: Norton.

Ferenczi, S. 1933. "The Confusion of Tongues Between Adults and Children: The Language of Tenderness and Passion." In M. Balint, ed., *Final Contributions to the Problems and Methods of Psycho-Analysis* 3:156–167. New York: Brunner/Mazel, 1980.

Flax, J. 1990. *Thinking Fragments: Psychoanalysis, Feminism, and Postmodernism in the Contemporary West*. Berkeley: University of California Press.

Fonagy, P. 1999. "Male Perpetrators of Violence Against Women: An Attachment Theory Perspective." *Journal of Applied Psychoanalytic Studies* 1, no. 1: 7–27.

Freud, A. 1966 [1936]. *The Ego and the Mechanisms of Defense*. Madison, Conn.: International Universities Press.

Freud, S. 1895. *Studies in Hysteria. The Standard Edition of the Complete Psychological Works of Sigmund Freud*, vol. 2. London: Hogarth.

—— 1920. *Beyond the Pleasure Principle. SE* 18:1–64.

—— 1923. *The Ego and the Id. SE* 19:1–66.

—— 1931. *Female Sexuality. SE* 21:221–243.

Geltner, P. 1995. Personal communication.

Gondolf, E. 1985. *Men Who Batter: An Integrated Approach for Stopping Wife Abuse*. Holmes Beach, Fla.: Learning.

Green, A. 1999. *The Work of the Negative*. London and New York: Free Association.

Greenson, R. 1967. *The Technique and Practice of Psychoanalysis*. Vol. 1. Madison, Conn.: International Universities Press.

Grotstein, J. 2000. *Who Is the Dreamer Who Dreams the Dream: A Study of Psychic Presences*. Hillsdale, N.J.: Analytic.

—— 2000. Personal communication.

Hartman, H. 1939. *Ego Psychology and the Problem of Adaptation*. New York: International Universities Press, 1958.

Joseph, B. 1987. "Projective Identification: Some Clinical Aspects." In M. Feldman and E. Spillius, eds., *Psychic Equilibrium and Psychic Change: Selected Papers of Betty Joseph*. London and New York: Tavistock/Routledge, 1989.

Khan, M. 1963. "The Concept of Cumulative Trauma." *The Privacy of the Self: Papers on Psychoanalytic Theory and Technique*. Madison, Conn.: International Universities Press, 1974.

Klein, M. 1940. "Mourning and Its Relation to Manic-Depressive States." In *Love, Guilt, and Reparation, and Other Works: 1921–1945*. Vol. 1. *The Writings of Melanie Klein*. New York: Free, 1975.

—— 1946. "Notes on Some Schizoid Mechanisms." In *Envy and Gratitude and Other Works: 1946–1963*. Vol. 3. *The Writings of Melanie Klein*. New York: Free, 1975.

Kohut, H. 1972. Thoughts on Narcissism and Narcissistic Rage. *The Psychoanalytic Study of the Child* 27: 360–400.

—— 1984. *How Does Analysis Cure?* Ed. A. Goldberg. Chicago: University of Chicago Press.

Langs, R. 1982. *The Psychotherapeutic Conspiracy*. New York: Aronson.

McDougall, J. 1995. *The Many Faces of Eros: A Psychoanalytic Exploration of Human Sexuality*. New York: Norton.

Mahler, M., F. Pine, and A. Bergman. 1975. *The Psychological Birth of the Human Infant: Symbiosis and Individuation*. New York: Basic.

Margolis, B. 1979. "Narcissistic Transference: The Product of Overlapping Self and Object Fields." *Modern Psychoanalysis*, 4, no. 2: 131–140.

—— 1981. "Narcissistic Transference: Further Considerations." *Modern Psychoanalysis*, 6, no. 2.

—— 1994 [1983]. "Joining, Mirroring, Psychological Reflection: Terminology, Definitions, Theoretical Considerations." *Modern Psychoanalysis*, 19, no. 2: 211–226.

Marshall, R. 1982. *Resistant Interactions: Child, Family, and Psychotherapist*. New York: Human Sciences.

Marshall, R. and S. Marshall. 1988. *The Transference-Countertransference Matrix: The Emotional-Cognitive Dialogue in Psychotherapy, Psychoanalyis, and Supervision*. New York: Columbia University Press.

Meadow, P. 1997. "Psychoanalysis and Violence." *Modern Psychoanalysis*, 22, no. 1:3–15.

Miller, A. 1983. *For Your Own Good: Hidden Cruelty in Child-Rearing and the Roots of Violence*. New York: Farrar, Straus, and Giroux.

Napier, A. and C. Whitaker. 1988. *The Family Crucible: The Intense Experience of Family Therapy*. New York: Perennial Library/Harper and Row.

Ogden, T. 1982. *Projective Identification and Psychotherapeutic Technique*. Northvale, N.J.: Aronson.

—— 1986. *The Matrix of the Mind: Objects Relations and the Psychoanalytic Dialogue*. Northvale, N.J.: Aronson.

Olds, S. 1999. "Leaving the Island." In S. Olds, *Blood, Tin, Straw*. New York: Knopf.

Pence, E. and M. Paymar. 1993. *Education Groups for Men Who Batter: The Duluth Model*. New York: Springer.

Racker, H. 1968. *Transference and Countertransference*. Madison, Conn.: International Universities Press.

Rycroft, C. 1968. *A Critical Dictionary of Psychoanalysis.* New York: Basic.

Scalia, J. 1994. "Psychoanalytic Insights and the Prevention of Pseudo-Success in the Cognitive-Behavioral Treatment of Batterers." *Journal of Interpersonal Violence* 9, no. 4: 548–555.

—— 1998. "A Psychoanalytic Perspective on Batterers." *Modern Psychoanalysis* 23, no. 1: 89–101.

Schoenewolf, G. 1993. *Counterresistance: The Therapist's Interference with the Therapeutic Process.* New York: Aronson.

Segal, H. 1973 [1964]. *Introduction to the Work of Melanie Klein.* 2d ed. New York: Basic.

—— 1977. *The Work of Hanna Segal.* New York: Aronson.

Shabad, P. 1993. "Repetition and Incomplete Mourning: The Intergenerational Transmission of Traumatic Themes." *Psychoanalytic Psychology* 10: 61–75.

Shur, R. 1994. *Countertransference Enactment: How Institutions and Therapists Actualize Primitive Internal Worlds.* New York: Aronson.

Sonkin, D., D. Martin, and L. Walker. 1985. *The Male Batterer: A Treatment Approach.* New York: Springer.

Spotnitz, H. 1985. *Modern Psychoanalysis of the Schizophrenic Patient.* New York: Human Sciences.

—— 1987 [1976]. *Psychotherapy of Preoedipal Conditions: Schizophrenia and Severe Character Disorders.* Northvale, N.J.: Aronson.

Stern, D. 1985. *The Interpersonal World of the Infant: A View from Psychoanalysis and Developmental Psychology.* New York: Basic.

Szollosy, M. 1998. "Winnicott's Potential Spaces: Using Psychoanalytic Theory to Redress the Crises of Postmodern Culture." Paper read at the Modern Language Association Convention, San Francisco, 1998.

Waelder, R. 1925. "The Psychoses: Their Mechanisms and Accessibility to Influence." *International Journal of Psychoanalysis* 37: 367–368.

Walker, L. 1979. *The Battered Woman.* New York: Harper and Row.

—— 1984. *Battered Woman Syndrome.* New York: Springer.

Winnicott, D. 1935. "The Manic Defence." In *Through Paediatrics to Psycho-Analysis: Collected Papers.* New York: Brunner/Mazel, 1958.

—— 1947. "Hate in the Countertransference." In *Through Paediatrics to Psycho-Analysis: Collected Papers.* New York: Brunner/Mazel, 1958.

—— 1954. "Metapsychological and Clinical Aspects of Regression Within the Psycho-Analytical Set-Up." In D. Winnicott, *Through Paediatrics to Psycho-Analysis: Collected Papers.* New York: Brunner/Mazel, 1958.

—— 1958. *Collected Papers.* London: Tavistock.

—— 1962. "Ego Integration in Child Development." In D. Winnicott, *The Maturational Processes and the Facilitating Environment.* Madison, Conn.: International Universities Press, 1965.

—— 1965. *The Maturational Processes and the Facilitating Environment.* Madison, Conn.: International Universities Press.

—— 1971. *Playing and Reality.* London: Routledge.

Wolf, E. 1988. *Treating the Self.* New York: Guilford.

INDEX